mid-May –	Jack Kennedy proposes to Jackie
June 24 –	Jackie's engagement to Jack is announced
Sept 12 –	Jackie marries Jack at St Mary's Church, Newport, Rhode Island

★ **1954**

Oct 11 –	Jack is admitted to hospital for lumbar fusion surgery

★ **1955**

Aug –	Jackie and Jack Kennedy attend a drinks party on Aristotle Onassis' yacht *Christina*, where Sir Winston Churchill was staying

★ **1956**

Aug 23 –	Jackie gives birth to a stillborn baby girl. She had also fallen pregnant in the first year of their marriage, but miscarried

★ **1957**

Aug 3 –	Black Jack Bouvier dies of cancer
Nov 27 –	Jackie gives birth to Caroline Bouvier Kennedy by cesarian section in the New York Lying-In Hospital, Cornell University Medical Center
Dec 13 –	Caroline is christened at St Patrick's Cathedral, New York

★ **1960**

Jan 2 –	Jack announces his candidacy for the Presidency of the USA
July 16 –	Jack wins Presidential nomination at the Democratic Party Convention, Los Angeles
Nov 6 –	John F. Kennedy is announced 35th President of USA
Nov 26 –	Jackie gives birth to John F. Kennedy Jr by cesarian section

★ **1961**

Jan 20 –	Jackie attends her husband's Presidential Inauguration Ceremony. The first instalment of Mary 'Molly' Van

July 11 –	Jackie stages an outdoor banquet in honor of President Ayub Khan of Pakistan at George Washington's former home, Mount Vernon, Virginia
Nov 13 –	Spanish cellist Pablo Casals plays at state dinner at the White House; he had vowed never to perform in the US because of the country's support for Franco
Dec 19 –	Jack's father Joseph Kennedy suffers a massive stroke

★ **1962**

Feb 14 –	CBS air the television special *A Tour of the White House with Mrs John F. Kennedy*
Mar 13 –	Jackie and Lee arrive in Delhi for their semi-official tour of India and Pakistan
May 11 –	Jackie assembles North America's finest artists and writers for a dinner in honor of French Minister for Culture Andre Malraux

★ **1963**

April 18 –	Jackie announces that she is pregnant.
Aug 7 –	Jackie is taken to hospital at the Otis Air Force base and gives birth prematurely to Patrick Bouvier Kennedy by cesarian section. He was born with hyaline membrane disease and died on 9 August in Boston's Children's hospital
Oct 4 –	Jackie joins her sister Lee on Aristotle Onassis' yacht *Christina* for a recuperative cruise
Nov 21 –	Jackie and Jack arrive in Texas for a campaigning visit
Nov 22 –	John F. Kennedy is assassinated in Dallas

the
Jackie
handbook

the
Jackie
handbook

**Naomi West
and Catherine Wilson**

MQP
MQ Publications Ltd

Jackie

Introduction

Jacqueline Bouvier Kennedy Onassis is a fascinating enigma, and the intrigue she provoked still endures over a decade after her death in 1994. The aura that remains is a potent distillate of her commanding style, her unfathomable personality and her drama-filled existence.

Jackie was an unusual and awe-inspiring human being. Although buffeted and assailed by appalling occurrences throughout her life, she persistently shaped the circumstances within her control with single-minded determination. Even while experiencing extremes of personal tumult in the immediate wake of John F Kennedy's assassination, Jackie gave precedence, not to her feelings, but to the crafting of a historical moment. It is this rare instinct which made her one of the most enthralling women of the 20th Century.

Born into the higher ranks of stratified East Coast society, Jackie had learned the importance of making a good marriage by the example of her ambitious mother—but her attitudes to men were defined by her rakish, womanizing father, whom she adored. She was drawn to powerful men, and following her father's advice the young Jackie adopted a geisha-like persona that belied her indomitable will and determination. She contrived a breathy, hushed speaking voice to lure people near, later described by Maria Callas as "Marilyn Monroe playing Ophelia." When Jackie elected to focus her undivided charm upon a fortunate recipient, they would find themselves bathed in its "dazzling brightness." She was (at very least) equally astute as the men around her, but recognized that her femininity was the seat of her power.

When she became America's First Lady, her unmatchable skills of self-presentation found full scope on a national and international stage. With each carefully choreographed move she had an unprecedented impact—she acquired enormous diplomatic importance through her encounters with international statesmen, she set a new standard with her pared-down sophisticated fashions, and she made America care about "good taste" by transforming a shabby White House into a proud, historically pertinent Executive Mansion. Most importantly, she purposefully suffused her youthful charisma with the dignity of a queen, and now remains treasured by America as the most perfect facsimile of royalty the country has ever had.

Yet, as the most famous woman in the world, Jackie became an expert at obscuring herself. In the White House she masked any signs of private tension—her bitten nails concealed beneath white gloves, her heavy smoking habit kept away from the gaze of cameras. She prized her role as mother above any of her public roles, and tried to bring up her children in private as much as possible.

But her reserve only made her all the more bewitching. That is what makes the search for the woman who became synonymous with her large, opaquely dark sunglasses an endless, but ultimately irresistible, challenge.

Note: All quotations are from Jackie Kennedy, unless otherwise indicated.

chapter 1

East Hampton
Idyll

To the manner born–1929 to 1951

Jacqueline Lee Bouvier was born in Southampton Hospital, Long Island, six weeks later than expected, on July 28, 1929. The 8-lb. girl was the first child of Janet Norton Lee, 22, and John Vernou Bouvier III, 38. Janet had been waiting out the long weeks until the baby's arrival at their New York home, but eventually decided to enjoy a Hamptons weekend at John Bouvier's father's twelve-acre estate, Lasata, where she went into labor.

Jackie's father, a stock specialist, had been one of New York's most notorious and desirable bachelors. He was tall and muscular with a scrupulously maintained year-round tan, which earned him such alternative monikers as "The Sheik," "The Black Prince," and, most often, "Black Jack." By the time Black Jack became romantically linked to the pretty Janet Lee, he had countless conquests and a number of broken engagements behind him. Bouvier's niece, Edie Beale, characterized their union as "fire and ice. Jack was divinely decadent and Janet was painfully proper."

Janet's family, the Lees, were newcomers to the ranks of moneyed New York society. Her grandparents were Irish immigrants and her father, James Thomas Lee, had made his fortune in property and finance, rising to become president and chairman of the board of the New York Central Savings Bank. According to Gore Vidal, he had changed his original Jewish name "Levy" to "Lee." The aspirant Janet referred to herself as one of "the Lees of Maryland" in an attempt to elevate her background to the level of one of the longer-established American lineages.

The Bouvier clan laid claim to rather grander French aristocratic roots, a claim published in 1925 by Jackie's grandfather, Major John Vernou Bouvier Jr., in a volume entitled *Our Forebears*. The Major traced their Bouvier ancestors back to François Bouvier, nobleman "of an ancient house of Fontaine near Grenoble." This account was held as Bouvier gospel until the early 1960s, when a historian worked out that the family had no links to the aristocratic Bouviers—only to a family of more lowly shopkeepers, farmers and artisans from a village near Arles.

Regardless of its complete lack of factual foundation, this assumed heritage was a defining element of the Bouvier outlook.

The Bouviers were poseurs. They looked like money, breeding, and power, but they weren't. Believing themselves to be aristocrats, they felt and behaved like aristocrats.

Truman Capote

Jackie's sister, Caroline Lee Bouvier, who was ever after known as Lee to please her "rather unpleasant" maternal grandfather, was born on March 3, 1933. The family lived between their eleven-room Manhattan apartment (in a Park Avenue building built and owned by James Lee) and East Hampton, where they spent each summer at Lasata and various Bouvier properties. Despite his heavy losses in the stock market crash of October 1929, Black Jack Bouvier continued to enjoy a luxurious lifestyle, assisted by loans. He employed a trainer, a masseuse, an English nanny, Bertha Newey, for his daughters, and two grooms for their stable at Lasata.

Black Jack and Janet were a well-known couple—throwing parties at the Devon Yacht Club, and organizing baseball games. Jackie first became socially prominent at the age of two, when her birthday made the social column of the *East Hampton Star.*

Lee looked back on these Long Island days with nostalgia. The sisters would eagerly anticipate the arrival of June each year, and another summer by the sea.

The idyll slowly dissolved. After the drawn-out disintegration of her turbulent marriage, Janet quickly sought out a more secure framework in which to raise her daughters. She married the wealthy Hugh D. Auchincloss Jr. (known as Hughdie) in 1942, a move which boosted them up the social pecking order. While they moved in elevated social circles in Newport, Rhode Island, where Hughdie had one of his grand homes, Hammersmith Farm, Jackie and Lee were keenly aware that, just like their mother, they would have to seek (or marry) their own fortune. As stepchildren, they did not stand to inherit any of Hughdie's money. The knowledge of this financial imperative would shape Jackie's every decision as she grew into an adult.

That was in my life, and I think in Jackie's as well, a really happy and far too brief time

Lee

Right: **Jackie and Janet in the garden of their East Hampton home, 1933** The Bouviers' world echoed many of the characteristics of English country life—featuring horses, dogs, cocktails, and a packed social calendar.

There's always been in her a kind of loneliness. Even as a young girl she created this incredible persona to protect herself and keep others at a ... distance.

Doris Kearns Goodwin

Left: **Jackie in her party dress photographed with her mother, Janet, 1932**

Next page: **Jackie with her baby sister, Caroline Lee Bouvier, 1933**
From birth, Jackie's sister was always called Lee as a mark of deference to Janet's wealthy family.

Family ambitions

The genteel East Hampton social season, punctuated by its frequent shows and gymkhanas, provided plentiful opportunities for Jackie's competitive streak to develop.

Her mother was a superb horsewoman, a "daredevil rider," who won scores of prizes herself and was Junior Master of the Suffolk Fox Hounds. Janet's physical courage and passion for riding were inherited by her eldest daughter. Jackie first sat on a horse when she was one, and competed regularly from the age of five. The determined Jackie would continually clamber back onto her horse, no matter how many times she was thrown off.

By the age of seven, Jackie had won two national championships and later, in 1940, another notable double achievement was reported in the the the *New York Times:* "Jacqueline Bouvier, an eleven-year-old equestrienne from East Hampton, Long Island, scored a double victory in the horsemanship competition. Miss Bouvier achieved a rare distinction. The occasions are few when a young rider wins both contests in the same show."

One member of the riding club observed that she often performed better when there was an appreciative audience—the entire Bouvier family could be relied upon to turn out, with Black Jack wearing an immaculate white gabardine suit and her grandfather, Grampy Jack, with his waxed mustache and pince-nez, wearing a Panama hat.

Right: **Janet, Jack and Jackie at the Smithtown Horse Show, Long Island, August 1933**
The Bouviers were prominent members of the horse show and riding set.

Black Jack and Janet kept four horses, including Jackie's favorite, Danseuse, and Lee's nemesis, the piebald Dancestep, who once reportedly rolled on top of Lee, nearly crushing her.

The daughter of Arthur Simmonds, Jackie's riding teacher, remembers that Jackie's aggressively competitive spirit finished Lee's interest in horseriding: "She was so intent on winning that she permanently soured her sister on the sport." Lee says that her father and Jackie would obsessively discuss Jackie's progress as a horsewoman. She remembers, "This horse, Danseuse, was the trio in their relationship for a good ten years."

As she grew up, riding became an essential release for Jackie. When she was seven years old, the family's East Hampton idyll began to disintegrate as Janet and Jack's relationship became increasingly antagonistic. Black Jack had failed to give up his prolific womanizing—even on the couple's honeymoon he enjoyed a flirtation with teenage tobacco heiress Doris Duke on board the SS *Aquitania*. But by the mid-1930s, his dalliances spelled increasing public humiliation for Janet. To add insult to Janet's injury, Jack's financial situation was slipping out of control and the family had become largely dependent on his father-in-law.

The Bouvier household became racked with tensions and explosive arguments as the highly strung Janet possessed a violent temper. Whenever a fight loomed, Jackie would be told to go and exercise her pony. Eventually, following a trial separation in 1936 and a temporary reunion in 1937, Janet divorced Jack in 1940.

Janet and her daughters moved to One Gracie Square—the girls would see their father for Sunday outings. Despite her young age at the time, Lee has clear recall of the sheer nastiness of her parents' break-up.

It was, of all the divorces I've heard about and watched, I think probably one of the very worst, because there was such relentless bitterness on both sides

Lee

Below: **Jack, Virginia Kernochan, and Janet, Tuxedo Horse Show, 1934**
This notorious photograph was published in the *New York Daily News*. Janet is sitting on a fence in her riding clothes, while Jack tenderly holds the hand of Virginia Kernochan, who is sitting between them.

She was a beautiful child, a replica of her father—the same wide-spaced, flashing eyes, dark coloration, prominent cheekbones

Judith Frame, Bouvier family friend

Left: **Jackie, pictured with one her dogs in the 1930s**
The Bouvier household incorporated a small crowd of adored dogs—
Jackie immortalized one of her favorites in a story, "*The Adventures of George Woofty, Esquire.*"

If Jackie happened to lose an event, her facial muscles would tighten into knots. Her mouth and jaw would pull tight as a rope. She wasn't happy unless she won, unless she beat all the other little kids.

Samuel Lester, who exercised horses at the East Hampton Riding Club

Right: **Jackie with her pony Buddy at the Sixth Annual Horse Show of Southampton Riding and Hunt Club, 1934**

Jackie was a courageous rider. If she was thrown while taking a jump, a moment later she'd scramble back on her horse.

Daddy's girl

"A most devastating figure" were the words Jackie chose to describe her own father. Lee and Jackie, nicknamed Pekes and Jacks, were doted on by Black Jack, and they idolized him in return. His physical charisma was such that he drew comparisons to movie stars and inevitably cut an exotic figure in East Hampton. As a reporter from the *East Hampton Star* related: "Mr. Bouvier is so deeply tanned with East Hampton sunshine that he much resembles one of those handsome Egyptians you see careening along in their Rolls Royce cars in Cairo, in the land of the Nile."

He was extremely vain, and his efforts to keep in shape included exercising in Central Park wearing a rubber suit. Black Jack's golf caddy remembers the particular attention he would pay to his hair:

"He must've used axle grease…because it was just about as slick and flat as you could get it."

Janet was the disciplinarian of the family, a critical perfectionist obsessed with social niceties. She took responsibility for keeping her girls in line while Jack would indulge his daughters at any opportunity—he allowed Jackie to keep a pet rabbit in the bath at their New York apartment. After the couple separated, this difference was further accentuated—the sisters' weekend visits with Black Jack were packed with shopping trips, zoo visits, and ice-cream sundaes. He would rent dogs from a pet shop for Jackie and Lee to walk through Central Park, and once took them to the Stock Exchange on Wall Street, to show them off to the traders—they were greeted with whoops and cheers.

Of his two daughters, it was Jackie to whom Black Jack directed the most intense affection. When he was doling out praise—or a dose of "vitamin P" as the family dubbed it—Jackie was often singled out for extra adulation: for her looks, her greater athleticism, and her intelligence. The bond between Jackie and Black Jack was exceptionally close. Jackie's cousin, John H. Davis, has said, "It was practically a love affair." A family friend noted that "she seemed to glow in his presence."

Her fun-loving, spirited personality seemed to have more in common with Black Jack's lively hedonistic soul than her mother's more rule-governed ways. As she grew to be a teenager, Jackie could not help but be aware of her father's predatory reputation (his encounters with scores of women were public knowledge and it was even rumored that he had a flirtation with Cole Porter). Descriptions of Black Jack's prowess with women were remarkably similar to later descriptions of John F. Kennedy.

"He could walk into a room full of women, and ninety-five percent of them wanted to be with him…Once he'd been with a woman he lost interest in her and moved onto the next," related Tom Collier, a contemporary of Black Jack at Yale.

But rather than disapproving of his Lothario behavior, Black Jack's frequently exercised power over the opposite sex just made Jackie love him all the more. She found his blatant lechery more amusing than embarrassing. Her friend John "Demi" Gates relates that when she was at school, "she'd say to him about the mothers of some of her friends, 'What about her?' and he'd say 'Yes, I've had her,' or he'd say 'No, but I think that's pretty imminent!' She thought that was wonderful."

They corresponded constantly throughout her formative years and on Jackie's visits to see him in New York, Black Jack would dispense advice about dealing with men—choice counsel such as "Play hard to get" and "All men are rats. Don't trust any of them."

Above: **Jackie and her mother, 1935**

Janet Lee Bouvier was admired for her flawlessly smart and stylish riding clothes, as well as her equestrian skills. With Jackie dressed in identical kit, mother and daughter won third prize in the family event at the East Hampton Show.

Right: **Jackie, 1935**

Black Jack's Harlequin Great Dane, King Phar, was feared by most adults in East Hampton, but Jackie had no such reservations. He was just one of the Bouvier family pets whom she proudly entered in local contests such as the annual Long Island Kennel Club Show.

I lived in New York City until I was thirteen and spent the summers in the country. I hated dolls, loved horses and dogs, and had skinned knees and braces on my teeth. I read a lot when I was little ... my heroes were Byron, Mowgli, Robin Hood, Little Lord Fauntleroy's grandfather, and Scarlett O'Hara.

Right: **Jackie, outside Miss Chapin's private school, on East End Avenue in New York, *circa* 1935**

Miss Chapin's was a predominantly WASP institution where she was one of the few Catholic pupils. Her class teacher described her as "full of the devil," and Jackie's naughtiness made her a frequent visitor to the office of the headmistress, Ethel Stringfellow. Miss Stringfellow commented: "I mightn't have kept Jacqueline, except that she had the most inquiring mind we'd had in the school in thirty-five years."

I like to use the word "original" in describing Jacqueline. She was very intense and felt strongly about things. She had enormous individuality and sensitivity and a marvelous self-control that perhaps concealed inner tensions.

Janet, Jackie's mother

Left: **Jackie, right, with her mother and Lee, 1939**
Several months later, Janet officially filed for divorce from Black Jack. Details of Black Jack's other women were detailed in the *New York Daily Mirror* of January 26, 1940 under the headline "Society Broker Sued for Divorce."

A brand new family

In the summer of 1942, the lives of Jackie and Lee were transformed by their mother's sudden second marriage—to Standard Oil heir Hugh D. Auchincloss Jr., known as Hughdie. He had been married twice before, first to a Russian naval officer's daughter, then to the willful alcoholic Nina Gore Vidal, mother of the writer Gore Vidal.

The stolid Hughdie was the polar opposite of the roguish Black Jack. Where Bouvier was extravagant, Auchincloss was tightfisted. He was renowned for drawn-out retellings of his favorite anecdotes, but was generally viewed with affection. And Hughdie's one vice—his extensive and diverse library of pornography—was, at least, not publicly enacted like Black Jack's vices.

The marriage meant a considerable step up in status for the Bouviers—Jackie enjoyed their new, grander life, living between Merrywood, a luxuriously appointed Georgian-style home in Virginia (where she took the bedroom recently vacated by Gore Vidal), and Hammersmith Farm, the Auchincloss estate near Newport, Rhode Island, which Hughdie inherited later in 1942.

Jackie enjoyed the company of her acquired siblings, particularly stepbrother Yusha, who was two years older. During the war, the pair helped in the running of Hammersmith Farm, which supplied the local naval base with food—Jackie would feed 2,000 chickens every morning, although she disliked it because "they were so mean to each other."

Right: **Jackie with (clockwise from top) Hugh Dudley "Yusha" Auchincloss III, Lee, Hugh D. Auchincloss Jr., Janet with baby Janet, Tommy Auchincloss and Nina Auchincloss, 1945**

Interview with Yusha Auchincloss
BELOVED STEPBROTHER AND BEST FRIEND
Hammersmith Farm, December 2004

Jackie was my best friend. We first met ten days after the bombing of Pearl Harbor in 1941. I thought she was beautiful. She was twelve years old. I wanted to marry Jackie. She was fascinated by everything. When we met, Jackie, Lee, and her mother were on Christmas vacation in Washington and I was fourteen years old. My father, who one year later married Jackie's mother, told me I was very lucky to have met Jackie and want to be with her, as in life we can choose our friends, but not often our family. I helped him to choose our new family. I was my father's best man at the wedding. Jackie and I remained close friends for the rest of our lives; she kept all my letters and I kept all of hers.

She was a sparkling, bright, and mischievous teenage girl. She had special qualities: she was perceptive from an early age, caring and courageous—whether she fell off her horse or had a wisdom tooth operation (when she decided to have all of her offending teeth out in one go). She always had a sense of duty and always wanted those around her to feel comfortable. I never saw her cry, only weep for others. I never heard or read of her complaining about herself.

She always thanked and often praised. She had the courage of her convictions: was determined, self-disciplined, and had a desire for perfection. Her capacity for concentration was exhibited by her love of storytelling, her drawing, and poetry, which were all fine from an early age. She was fun, but never cruel. Her humor was often directed at herself. Her praise—when earned—was often lavish. She would stamp her foot, clap her hands, point her finger, and then hug. She could see through deception, faint flattery, or false pride: her reaction to all of these was usually swift and not subtle. One had to earn her confidence, and once earned, continue to deserve it. As a perfectionist, she had high standards. Her concern for you was mixed with compassion. And those on the receiving end of her love always felt fortunate and their lives enriched.

We grew up together, living at Hammersmith Farm and Merrywood, and shared a passion for both places. Merrywood was a sort of heaven. Hammersmith Farm, where I still live today, was her favorite place in the world—she used to say.

She was always a great reader, and knew and loved stories. She was very romantic, and as a girl she thought of herself as Scarlett O'Hara. She loved her father a great deal and worshipped him. She liked to think of him as a pirate. She always loved to tease and was a great rider, much better than me. I had a polo pony called Chief and she had a favorite called Danseuse. Before she brought Danseuse to Merrywood, I gave her half of my horse. Her comment was typical of her wit: she looked at me and said: "Do I have the back half so I have to clean up, or the front half so I have to buy the food?"

When we were teenagers and began dating, we helped each other. We had our "intelligence gathering system" when I would introduce her to friends of mine at Yale where I was studying, and if she did not have an escort to a dance, I would take her. Jackie was a wonderful dancer and we used to mimic Fred and Ginger and tap dance. She was a very beautiful debutante, but chaste."

Next page: **Jackie with her horse Danseuse, outside Miss Porter's school in Farmington, Connecticut, which she attended from 1944**
On her graduation from Miss Porter's, her yearbook entry read "Ambition: Not to be a housewife."

New worlds, broader horizons

Jackie spent her teens at a girls' boarding school, Miss Porter's in Farmington, Connecticut. Among her wealthy fellow pupils, her own financial situation was driven home—she lived grandly as part of the Auchincloss world, but none of Hughdie's fortune was destined to come to her or Lee.

From Farmington, Jackie went to Vassar, the all-girls' college in Poughkeepsie, 78 miles from New York City. Although she scored high grades at the college, she was clearly looking beyond the confines of "that goddamn Vassar," where she felt like a "schoolgirl among schoolgirls." She dated widely, mostly college students, some of whom were friends of Yusha, then at Yale. She was not given to gossip with girlfriends about her chaste experiences with men—one date recalled, "You were lucky to get a peck on the cheek." None of her attachments at that time seemed particularly important to her. The process of dating was rather more a means of perfecting her charm; of refining her powers over men. Her nascent method has been compared to that of an "American geisha"; speaking in a soft, unintimidating voice, she would pay the subject her undivided attention. George Plimpton said, "She had a wonderful way of looking at you and enveloping you with this gaze. Never looking over your shoulder and seeing who's coming up next."

After her first year at Vassar, instead of spending the summer with Black Jack (whose gambling and drinking problems were worsening), she went on a trip to Europe with Helen and Judy Bowdoin and Julia Bissell. The Bowdoins' stepfather, then a minister in the British government, inveigled an invitation to the Queen's Buckingham Palace garden party, where Jackie queued twice over to shake Sir Winston Churchill's hand in the reception line.

This taste of Europe spurred her to return—and she applied for the Smith College Junior Year Abroad program at the Sorbonne, winning a place to spend a year in Paris. There she lived with the aristocratic, but poor, de Renty family. Her contacts gave her access to high social circles and soon, alongside pursuing her studies "swaddled in sweaters and woolen stockings doing homework in graph-paper cahiers," Jackie was part of a world of "glamour, glitter, and rush." She relished the cultural life of Paris, visiting the Louvre, the theater, the ballet, and going to underground cafes and jazz bars on the back of a Bohemian artist's motorcycle. Her European year was completed with a fun-packed three-week jaunt around Ireland and Scotland with her stepbrother Yusha.

On her return, she enrolled at the George Washington University in Washington D.C. to complete her major in French Literature. While finishing her course, she entered the *Vogue Prix de Paris* writing competition, held annually—the winner won a year-long contract with the magazine, six months in New York, and six in Paris. Jackie carefully typed her entry, which included an essay on "People I Wish I Had Known" (those being Sergei Diaghilev, Charles Baudelaire, and Oscar Wilde) and a droll personal profile that read:

"As to physical appearance, I am tall, 5 ft.7 in., with brown hair, a square face, and eyes so unfortunately far apart that it takes three weeks to have a pair of glasses made with a bridge wide enough to fit over my nose."

Jackie beat 1,280 other entrants and had her portrait taken by Horst P. Horst. Despite her delight at winning, she did not spend long at *Vogue*. Jackie quickly realized that a fashion magazine in New York was not the best place to enhance her marriage prospects. In the fall of 1951, she moved back to Merrywood in Virginia, prepared to become a central part of Washington life.

I passed the finish line when I learned to smoke, in the balcony of the Normandie Theater in New York, from a girl who pressed a Longfellow on me, then led me from the theater when the usher told her that other people could not hear the film with so much coughing going on

Left: **Jackie, 1945**
The sixteen-year-old Jackie saw the acquisition of a smoking habit as a key rite of passage into sophisticated adulthood.

I loved it more than any year
of my life. Being away from home
gave me a chance to look at myself
with a jaundiced eye.
I learned not to be ashamed of
a real hunger for knowledge,
something I had always
tried to hide.

Left: Jackie sets sail with fellow students on the Junior Year Abroad
program, bound for the Sorbonne in Paris, August 24, 1949

Lee was the beauty, but Jackie had the spark and the brains

Vivian Stokes Crespi, Newport friend

Right: **Jackie with Lee, photographed by Cecil Beaton, 1951**

That year the sisters spent the summer charming their way around Europe. Jackie was already established as a top debutante—society columnist Igor Cassini had named her "Queen Debutante of the Year1947." She and Lee went to Pamplona for the bull-running festival, and also visited Venice and Florence. While in Florence they met the art critic Bernard Berenson at his nearby villa. He dispensed advice to the pair: "Marry someone who will constantly stimulate you—and you him."

chapter 2

Love
Marriage
Destiny

A dream come true–1952 to 1960

When she returned from Europe to Merrywood, Virginia, twenty-two-year-old Jacqueline Bouvier decided to start a career in journalism in the US capital. Her stepfather Hughdie spoke to his friend Arthur Krock, head of the *New York Times*' Washington office, who asked Frank Waldrop, editor of the *Washington Times-Herald*: "Are you still hiring little girls?", suggesting that he hire the "round-eyed, clever" Jackie.

Jackie began work at the paper as an all-purpose gofer, then rose to the position of receptionist. When Waldrop decided to launch a column produced by a full-time roving reporter/photographer, Jackie put herself up for the job of Inquiring Camera-Girl, despite her very limited experience in both reporting and photography.

Being a journalist seemed the ideal way of both having a job and experiencing the world, especially for anyone with a sense of adventure

For the feature, she would roam the entire city of Washington turning the Speed Graflex camera, which she had learned to use on a crash course, on an intriguingly wide range of subjects—from truck drivers and circus clowns to senators and their wives. She grilled Pat Nixon, for instance, and quizzed celebrities such as actress Tallulah Bankhead. For a salary of $56.75 per week, she posed alternately droll and searching questions such as: "Do you think bikini bathing suits are immoral?" and "Do you think the rich enjoy life more than the poor?"

Jackie found working in newspapers stimulating, and wrote gushingly to reporter Bess Armstrong in 1952: "I think I look up to newspaper people the way you join movie star fan clubs when you're ten years old." This sentiment contrasts sharply with her later antipathy to reporters, after she became a public figure.

Perhaps most rewarding for Jackie was the experience of being fully involved in Washington life. She became increasingly fascinated by the politics and history in which the city is steeped—she worked on a proposal for a historical television documentary about the Octagon House where President James Madison and his wife Dolly lived when the White House was burned in 1812.

By 1952, she had started to develop her own political opinions, which diverged from her Republican upbringing. "You have to be a Republican to realize how nice it is to be a Democrat," she said. During the 1952 presidential race, she was "Mad for Adlai"—the urbane Democratic candidate, Adlai Stevenson—even though she still had not registered to vote.

Jackie's closest social circle in Washington mostly consisted of people older than her—there was Charlie Bartlett, the Washington correspondent for the *Chattanooga Times*; John B. White, a former *Times-Herald* writer who worked for the Department of State; and Bill Walton, who had been the star war correspondent at *Time-Life*. When her mother and stepfather were away she would hold parties at Merrywood, inviting Washington bigwigs two generations older than herself.

All the while, her prospects for marriage were uppermost in Jackie's mind. Over the Christmas of 1951, she had gone so far as to get engaged to John Husted, a handsome WASP banker. He was entranced by her, describing her as "like a deer that had suddenly emerged from the forest and seen its first human being."

But Jackie soon got cold feet about the union. Janet's enthusiasm also waned when she discovered that Husted only made a salary of $17,000 per year. In March 1952, she broke off the engagement, wordlessly slipping the ring into Husted's suit jacket pocket at the end of a visit.

Jackie's first encounter with John F. Kennedy (known as Jack), a wealthy congressman, was at a dinner party organized by Charlie Bartlett and his wife Martha, before she went on her summer trip to Europe in 1951. Jack was impressed by her, and as he recalled, he "leaned across the asparagus and asked her for a date." (Jackie later pointed out that the Bartletts did not serve asparagus that night.) But it was not until May 8 the following year, at another Bartlett dinner party, that the relationship between Jack and Jacqueline Lee Bouvier became something more serious. One of her biographers recorded the moment: "She realized that here was a man who did not want to marry … in that revealing moment she envisaged heartbreak, but just as swiftly determined that heartbreak would be worth the pain."

The pair began to date in a "spasmodic" fashion while he traveled all over Massachusetts campaigning for the senatorship. But as time went on, Jackie made a more concerted effort to secure this bachelor whose attraction was such that women "were drawn to him in the battalions, by the brigades," as writer Gloria Emerson put it. After he was elected senator in November, she began to show her potential worth as a mate—she took him hot lunches in his office and translated ten French books on Southeast Asian politics to help him write his first speech. In her "Inquiring Camera-Girl" column, she started to use questions that reflected her preoccupations: "Can you give me any reason why a contented bachelor should get married?"; "The Irish author Sean O'Faolain claims that the Irish are deficient in the art of love. Do you agree?"

In mid-May, 1953, Jack Kennedy proposed to Jackie. He had been helped in his decision by the approval of his multimillionaire father, Joseph P. Kennedy. On visits to the tight-knit, highly competitive Kennedy clan at their Massachusetts home, Hyannis Port, Jackie had been confronted by the barely veiled suspicions of Jack's formidable sisters—Patricia, Jean, and Eunice—who nicknamed her "The Deb" and poked fun at her "Babykins" voice. But, importantly, Joe Kennedy was charmed by her wit and beauty, and impressed by her strength of character. He told his wife Rose:

She's the only one around here with any gumption

Joe Kennedy

Jackie did not provide Jack with an immediate response to his proposal, instead heading to Britain for two weeks to witness the coronation of Queen Elizabeth II, which she covered for the Times-Herald ("ARTICLES EXCELLENT, BUT YOU ARE MISSED," Jack cabled). She went on to spend a further two weeks in Paris, where Gore Vidal reports that "she lost her virginity to a friend of mine in a lift that he had stalled in a pension on Paris's Left Bank." Vidal says that the lovers discussed Jackie's intention to marry Jack, she explaining her choice simply: "He has money and you don't."

She flew back on June 14, landing in Boston, where Jack was there to meet her, and gave him her answer.

As soon as Jackie had accepted Jack's proposal, the Kennedy family immediately began preparing a wedding that would be a media event of a magnitude to equal their towering political ambitions for Jack.

Neither Janet nor Jackie herself desired a big, showy wedding, considering it vulgar, but Jack, Rose, and Joe Kennedy put all their efforts into persuading them otherwise.

Look, Mrs. Auchincloss, your daughter is marrying a political figure ... There are going to be photographers whether we like it or not.

Jack Kennedy

The *New York Times* reported that three thousand onlookers gathered outside St. Mary's Church in Newport and knocked over police cordons in order to see the happy couple better. Jackie complied with the Kennedys' demands even to the point of choosing a particularly traditional dress, rather than a more modern and simple style. But even aside from the overblown production, the day was not to be without trauma for Jackie. Her father, Black Jack, was set to give her away. However, Janet had been doing her utmost to exclude him from all the pre-wedding events—a string of cocktail parties and dinners. By the morning of the wedding, Black Jack had reacted to the continuing wranglings over his part in proceedings by getting drunk at his hotel. Janet promptly banned him from the church and Hughdie stepped in as substitute. Jackie managed to hide her bitter upset, but wrote to Black Jack from her honeymoon, a letter of understanding and forgiveness.

Having secured her financial future by marrying into the Kennedy family, Jackie was quickly forced to learn the demands that the situation would make upon her in return. Jack was frequently on the campaign trail and she had to learn how to behave in the face of his constant philandering. She took a realistic line: "I don't think there are any men who are faithful to their wives. Men are such a combination of good and evil."

But despite a number of trials—her difficulties bearing a child, and Jack's brush with death following a back operation—Jackie survived the early years of marriage to a Kennedy with aplomb. As a politician's wife she lacked the common touch ("too much status and not enough quo" as Jack described her), but did not compromise her cultured nature when she joined him on the campaign trail. Yet still, Jackie had a powerful draw that matched Jack's own, and went on to help him achieve his greatest triumph, winning the presidency. Joe Kennedy's endorsement of this witty, soft-spoken society girl had been proved resoundingly right. She had the mettle to make a First Lady.

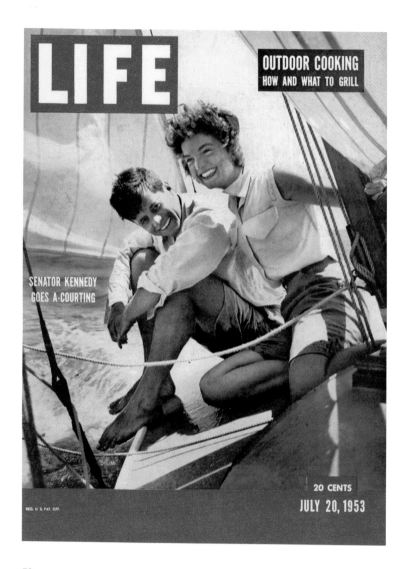

LIFE

OUTDOOR COOKING
HOW AND WHAT TO GRILL

SENATOR KENNEDY
GOES A-COURTING

20 CENTS

JULY 20, 1953

At that point in my life, what I wanted more than anything else in the world was to be married to him

Left: **Jack and Jackie on the cover of *LIFE* magazine, July 20, 1953, photographed sailing off Cape Cod, Massachusetts**

Only days after their engagement had been announced on June 24, and Jack had given her a twinned square-cut emerald and diamond ring from Van Cleef and Arpels, Joe Kennedy invited a photographer from *LIFE* magazine to spend three days at the Kennedy home at Hyannis Port. Jackie was shocked at the idea, but the Kennedy family convinced her it would help Jack's career. The photographer took hundreds of photographs of the betrothed couple for a story entitled "Senator Kennedy Goes A-Courting."

I took the choicest bachelor in the Senate

Right: **Jackie and Jack photographed in the Kennedy family living room at Hyannis Port, July 1953**

Jackie and the Kennedy clan

When Jackie began her courtship with Jack, she was, unavoidably, embarking on a relationship with the entire Kennedy family. The Kennedy clan en masse were a redoubtable force—at their head was their patriarchal father, Joseph P. Kennedy, a businessman who, having amassed an inexhaustible fortune (partly through importing "medicinal" whisky during Prohibition), was now shaping and driving the ambitions of the offspring he produced with his wife, Rose. Besides Jack, Jackie was to acquire three sisters: Eunice, Patricia, and Jean, and two brothers: Bobby and Teddy. Rose Kennedy said of her own family:

"The Kennedys were like a nation unto themselves with their own private language and customs. They invited friends into their lives, but there was always a distance between them."

Despite Joe Kennedy's immense wealth and the status it accorded them, the Kennedys were not socially gregarious as a family—they were much more inward-looking, ruled principally by their intense family loyalties. The closeness of their bonds seemed near incestuous at times—the Kennedy men, including Joe (who was a womanizer to eclipse Jackie's own father, Black Jack), would pass women on to one another.

"All those Kennedy men are the same—they're like dogs, they have to stop and pee on every fire hydrant," said Truman Capote.

The Kennedys might have shared an unassailable confidence from being part of this unit, but they had also been collectively rocked by a series of tragedies—Joe and Rose's eldest son, Joe Jr., died in 1944 on a secret bombing mission during World War II, then their daughter Kathleen "Kick" Kennedy died in an air crash over France in 1948. Their mentally unstable eldest daughter Rosemary was institutionalized in a convent in Wisconsin, having been subjected to a prefrontal lobotomy in 1941.

Joining the whole family for the first time at their white-painted house on Cape Cod in 1952, Jackie was overwhelmed by their relentless competitive activity—days were filled with physical games, touch football, swimming, softball, tennis, and then conversation round the dinner table would be no less competitive.

Jack's sisters regarded her as an intruder, and tested her resilience by teasing and undermining her rarified ways. When she tried to get them to call her by her full name, pronounced "Jaclean," Eunice, who has been described as a female version of Jack, replied under her breath, "Rhymes with 'queen.'" Their boisterous behavior was hardly on Jackie's wavelength, and in return she dubbed them the "toothy girls" and the "rah-rah girls."

The Kennedy women would stop at nothing to advance Jack's career, and indeed had been instrumental in securing Jack's seat in the Senate. His opponent Henry Cabot Lodge blamed his defeat by Jack on the Irish Catholic women's vote, which had been mobilized effectively by tea parties held by Rose and her daughters. "It was those damn teas that killed me," Cabot Lodge said.

The difference between Jackie and others who married into the Kennedy clan was that she did not want to be subsumed and conform to their ways—she was desperate to keep her own identity rather than morphing into an honorary Kennedy. Jackie could not have been more different than Bobby's wife, the wisecracking, rambunctious Ethel, who was such a perfect fit with the other Kennedys that she was described as "more Kennedy than thou."

Rather than kowtowing to Rose, Jackie instinctively appealed to Joe for his approval as a wife for Jack. She found Joe charming, and he in turn was bewitched by her.

Jackie was outspoken. "She cajoled him, teased him, talked back to him," remembers Jack's close friend Lem Billings. Jackie also took care to hint at her elevated social background to give Joe the impression that Jack would be marrying up. Thus Jackie had won her trump card. "A Catholic politician has to have a Catholic wife," Joe said. "She should have class. Jackie probably had more class than any girl we've ever seen around here."

She was worried about being taken over by politics and another family, because she always wanted to be herself, and I think that losing her own personality was what she was most worried about

Aileen Bowdoin Train, friend

Right: **Jack and Jackie playing baseball for the benefit of the *LIFE* photographer, Hyannis Port, July 1953**

Jackie made the effort to join in with the Kennedy's compulsive game-playing, and was observed to be a "gazelle-like" presence amongst the Kennedy rough-and-tumble. She spoke disparagingly of the family's relentless physical activity to her sister Lee: "When they have nothing else to do, they run in place. Other times they fall all over each other like a pack of gorillas."

Interview with Jamie Auchincloss

JACKIE'S HALF BROTHER

Ashland, Oregon, December 2004

Jackie was my big half sister. She was seventeen years older than me and we shared the same mother. I was christened on the day of her coming-out party at Hammersmith Farm, one of our homes. My earliest memory of Jackie is carrying her train on her wedding day when I was six-and-a-half, in September 1953.

I was a page, and I remember the wedding was a big deal. Twelve hundred guests were coming to the reception at home after the service in St. Mary's Church. Jackie didn't have a very good day. Her father, Jack Bouvier, had come up from New York to give her away. The divorce between him and my mother was quite bitter. It was unusual in those days to get divorced and it meant excommunication from the church. So my mother made life very difficult for her former husband on Jackie's wedding day: she would not have him in the house, so he was put up at a hotel downtown. She instructed the ushers to make sure the hotel kept room service going twenty-four hours a day, as she knew Jack (in his nervous state) would drink on his own or invite people over, and then would not be in a fit state to give Jackie away at the wedding.

To get Jack drunk was one of the assignments my mother gave to my half brother Yusha and Michael Canfield, who had just married my sister Lee. Both of them were told to ply Jack with

Right: **Jamie as page boy at Jack and Jackie's wedding, Hammersmith Farm, September 12, 1953**

Jamie is standing at Jack's side, with Lee's hand on his shoulder.

alcohol. I was too young at the time to understand, but I know this is what happened as they both told me when I was older.

I was aware that Jackie was pretty tense. She figured out what my mother had done and was very upset. Jack Bouvier finally came to the wedding late, and sat in the back row. My mother would not allow him to come to the reception afterwards. Jackie went up the aisle on the arm of my father [Hugh Auchincloss], who I think had the whole thing planned with my mother beforehand. He was all ready to do it, and had a coat put away for the event. The tension spread to others: even when the wedding photographs were being taken I remember the pecking orders and jealousies within the two families coming out, with our mother trying to control them all.

I was very fortunate to have Jackie as an older sister—she behaved like a substitute mother. She always liked the role of mother and practiced it from an early age. There were many things she admired about our mother, but she learned to keep a distance from her as she could be very imperious and formal.

Jackie was remarkably casual and informal: she thought children should not have to act as grown-ups and shared her wicked sense of humor with us. She was always a lot of fun. She would tell us about the pranks she used to get up to when she was at Miss Porter's school. Jackie was known for putting Vaseline on the staff toilet bowls so when a teacher sat down she would not remain stable. My mother would be called in by the headmistress and told that they had an exceptionally bright and creative student in Jackie, but I remember my mother despairing at how hard she sometimes was to control.

In those days it was considered better for women to not have so many brains if they wanted to marry easily. She was schooled to become a wife and a mother but always rebelled when she was told off and claimed she wanted a more bohemian life. Yet however much she claimed she wanted an independent and unconventional way of life as a young woman, most of the time she would not do anything untoward and had very good manners.

Our mother brought us all up very strictly. She was a woman of her time which meant that she was only really comfortable with people who she thought were in her own class, and she wanted that class to be as high possible. Every person she knew and wanted us to know would have to be of her race and economic status. A lot of people called her a social climber, which she was. She was of Irish Catholic stock, but pretended that she was an English Catholic. Both she and Jack Bouvier came from families that had padded their genealogical résumé.

Our mother wanted everything her own way. My father, Hugh Auchincloss, was very laid back and did not like any confrontation at all. He left all the disciplining and organization of us children to my mother, which she enjoyed almost too much. The houses we lived in were very much her houses. She had quite a temper and if you did not say sorry to her immediately, she would get angrier and angrier, which could be very frightening.

Jackie always knew how to handle her: she would just walk away. Janet took a lot of pills and did not drink much water and when cocktail hour came round those daiquiris of hers could be very large. Dinner was meant to be at seven-thirty and often we did not sit down to eat until nine, when the food would be cold. Jackie and I and the rest of the family dreaded it when she had been drinking.

She had these huge orb-shaped glasses which she would spill the more she drank, yet still managed to hold together a great conversation with that arched voice of hers. I remember sipping one of her drinks once; it was bitter—you could smell the alcohol on her from two feet away.

It was one of those "perfect" weddings—a sunny, windswept day, horses and cattle grazing in the pastures, everybody radiant and fit

Eilene Slocum, wedding guest

Left: **Jackie with a group of her bridesmaids, September 12, 1953**
Her matron-of-honor was Lee Bouvier Canfield. Her maid-of-honor was
Nina Auchincloss and her flower girl was Janet Auchincloss. Her bridal
attendants were Nancy Tuckerman, Martha Bartlett, Ethel Skakel
Kennedy, Jean Kennedy, Shirley Oakes, Aileen Travers, Sylvia Whitehouse,
and Helen Spaulding

She later told her friend, fashion designer Carolina Herrera, that she
had not liked her wedding dress, made by New York dressmaker Ann
Lowe. Jackie would have preferred something simpler and more modern,
but Jack had requested "something traditional and old-fashioned."

Next page: **Jackie and Jack's wedding breakfast, September 12, 1953**
There was a reception for over 1,300 guests. They enjoyed creamed
chicken and slices from a four-foot-high wedding cake, and later danced to
music from the Meyer Davis Band.

The new Mrs Kennedy

After the couple's Acapulco honeymoon, the young Senator and Mrs. Kennedy's married life had a less than desirable start. They lived "like gypsies" for months, mostly staying at Hyannis Port, where Jackie was forced to fall in with her mother-in-law's routines.

"I longed for a home of our own. I hoped it would give our lives some roots, some stability," Jackie recalled.

By January, they had found a home to rent temporarily in Georgetown, Washington D.C., and Jackie could start conducting her wifely duties. "I thought the best thing I could do was to be a distraction. Jack lived and breathed politics all day long. If he came home to more table-thumping, how could he ever relax?" she said.

They were both voracious readers and would constantly exchange books—history, fiction, or poetry. Jackie also encouraged Jack to paint, convincing him that it was a macho hobby as it was pursued by his hero, Sir Winston Churchill. She enrolled in an American history course (which included a class in political courage) at Georgetown University, in order to be better informed.

But for Jackie it was a lonely time—Jack was never home more than two nights in a row. "Politics was sort of my enemy, and we had no home life whatsoever," she said, and she had to begin to accept his continuing liaisons with other women as a fact of life.

There were yet worse tests for Jackie—during their first year of marriage her first pregnancy miscarried, and in October 1954, she had to face the prospect of losing Jack. He had undergone a double spinal fusion operation to solve the chronic back pain he suffered, but due to his other health problems—an adrenal deficiency and Addison's disease—he succumbed to postoperative infection, which nearly killed him. A priest was called to read the last rites. Jackie was at his side throughout seven months of slow recovery, dressing his infected wound several times a day, bringing him magazines and newspapers, responding to well-wishers. She also did initial research for a book about historical political figures, *Profiles in Courage*, which Jack put together as he convalesced. It went on to win a Pulitzer Prize.

By 1956, Jack was campaigning at full pelt for the vice-presidential nomination, and Jackie was pregnant again. Despite being in the final weeks of pregnancy, she attended the Democratic Convention in Chicago in August, and later that month she had a stillborn baby girl. She unofficially named her Arabella. Jack was away sailing off the coast of Italy at the time, having just lost the vice-presidential nomination, and only returned five days after Jackie had given birth. Jack proved deficient when it came to dealing with Jackie's fluctuating emotions. "We didn't fully understand each other," he said.

Rumors began to circulate that their marriage was breaking down, and even that Joe Kennedy had offered Jackie a million dollars not to divorce Jack at this vital period in his career. However, the dark clouds of unhappiness surrounding the Kennedy union were dissipated by the arrival of the robustly healthy baby, Caroline Bouvier, on November 27, 1957. Jackie now had a family and a home—3307 N Street in Washington, which she had stylishly redecorated. The following year, she applied herself to assisting Jack's successful campaign to be reelected as senator, visiting every district of Massachusetts. To the Kennedy clan and the American public, Jackie's true political worth was now beginning to become plain.

Above: **Jackie preparing for her first dinner party, May, 1954**
As *McCall's* magazine noted, "Jackie's no cook, but she sets a fine table, will take ten, but prefers six, at her dinners." In May 1954, photographer Orlando Suero spent five days with the Kennedys at their rented Georgetown home, 3321 Dent Place, photographing them for a story on Jackie for the magazine.

Right: **Jackie takes her poodle for a walk in Washington, May, 1954**
Jackie's passion for dogs (and horses) continued into her marriage.

Above: **Jackie with Jack in his Senate office, May, 1954**
"This was a real working session ... It wasn't set up for the camera. Jackie
was helping him read and edit materials," remembers Orlando Suero,
the photographer.

I brought a certain order to Jack's life. He no longer went out in the morning with one brown and one black shoe on

Above: **Jackie and Jack in their garden, May, 1954**
Jackie introduced her husband to the pleasures of painting early on in their relationship—and he took to it with typical Kennedy energy and enthusiasm.

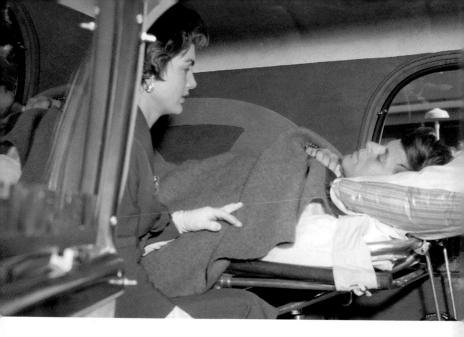

Above: **Jackie with Jack in an ambulance on December 21, 1954**
They went to Joe Kennedy's Palm Beach home to recuperate from Jack's
spinal operation, after which he had contracted a life-threatening infection
"My wife is a pretty shy, quiet girl, but when things get rough she can
handle herself pretty well," Jack said.

Right: **Jackie leaving New England Baptist Hospital, November 18, 1955**
She had broken her right ankle in one of the Kennedys' touch football
games at Hyannis Port

Five years later, just before Jack Kennedy took presidential office, the
magazine *Sports Illustrated* recalled the incident as a badge of honor for
Jackie: "Jacqueline Kennedy will be the first First Lady who ever broke an
ankle playing football."

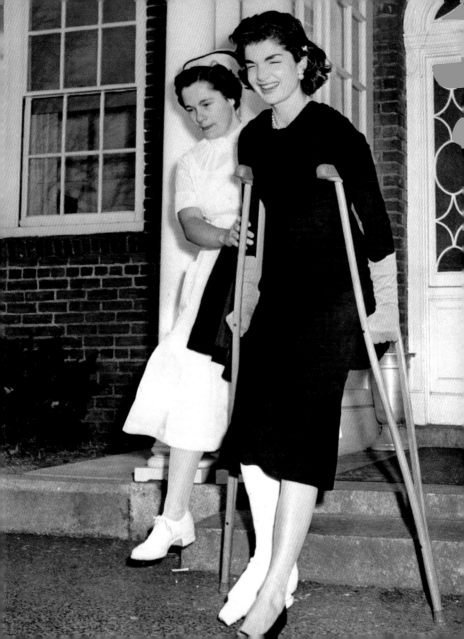

Mrs. John F. Kennedy plans her clothes to a well-liked minimum, often with year-round fashions for Washington and Georgetown, where she and her husband live

Ladies Home Journal

Left and above: **Jackie modeling stylish clothes, ranging from casual wear to glamorous evening gowns,** *Ladies' Home Journal,* **1957**

There were Jack's sisters, always bragging about how much capital the family controlled, how powerful Joe was ... and how Jack would be elected president in 1960. They undoubtedly drove Jackie crazy, and she probably drove them up the wall as well.

Senator George Smathers

Above: **Jackie with the Kennedy sisters May 1956**
From left: to right, Patricia Lawford, Bobby's wife Ethel Kennedy, Jean
Kennedy Smith, and Eunice Kennedy Shriver. They are at a party being
held in honor of Jean Kennedy Smith,

How young she was, and how different from all the rest of us

Lady Bird Johnson, wife of Senator Lyndon Baines Johnson

Left: **Jackie and Jack attending a dinner at the Senate Office Building, Washington DC, 1956**

Jackie knew that her youth, style, and elevated cultural interests inevitably set her apart from the other politicians' wives. "She couldn't tolerate those women. She made fun of their dowdiness and slobbering devotion to their husbands' political careers. 'They're such pigeons,' she used to say."

Above: **Jackie, pregnant with Caroline, walking on the beach with Bobby, Ethel, and Jack near Joe Kennedy's estate at Palm Beach, Florida, July 19, 1957**

Earlier in the summer, Jackie had flown to New York to see her father but was unaware that he was seriously ill with liver cancer. Black Jack slipped into a coma on August 3, before Jackie could fly to see him, and died on August 5.

The one who I would put my hand in the fire for.

Jackie, on Bobby Kennedy

Below: **Jackie and Jack at Bobby and Ethel's home, Hickory Hill, near Merrywood in Virginia, with their son, Joseph Jr., June 1957**
Jackie and Jack had originally bought Hickory Hill for themselves in October 1955, but after the stillbirth of their child in August 1956, Jackie could not face returning there, and they sold it to Bobby and Ethel.

I'll always remember Jack's face when the doctor came into the waiting room and told him that the baby had arrived ... I don't remember that he said anything. But I just remember his sweet expression and a sort of smile.

Janet, Jackie's mother

Left: **Jackie at the christening of Caroline Bouvier Kennedy, at St. Patrick's Cathedral, New York, December 13, 1957**
Archbishop Richard Cushing christened Caroline, who wore Jackie's christening robe. Her godparents were Bobby Kennedy and Jackie's sister Lee, now Mrs. Michael Canfield.

For Jackie, being a mother seemed to validate her sense of self. It gave her an inner peace and security which nothing else ever had. It opened her heart.

Doris Kearns Goodwin

Right: **Jackie with Caroline at their Georgetown home, March 1958**
Jackie allowed a photographer from *LIFE* to have access to the nursery to support Jack in his reelection campaign effort, but such a move was against her better judgment. She fiercely guarded Caroline's privacy.

Next page: **Jackie with Caroline at the Kennedys' summer home in Hyannis Port, August 21, 1959**
Jackie talked about Caroline's precocious intelligence in much the same way as Janet used to describe hers when she was very young: "She talks about *Le Roi Soleil* as if he were Peter Rabbit."

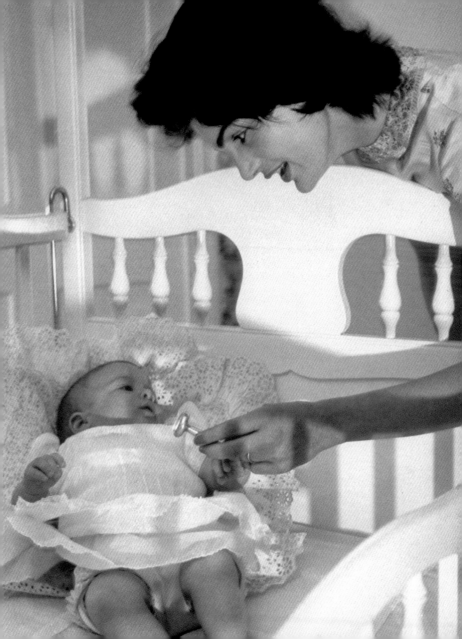

The candidate's wife

There had been concerns expressed within the Kennedy camp that Jackie's highbrow, glamorous image would not cut much ice with the average American voter. Indeed, some of her habits on the campaign trail might have compounded such worries—whilst traveling in a motorcade she had been observed reading Proust or de Gaulle's memoirs.

One particular liability was Jackie's choice of fashions. Jackie had a penchant for exclusive Paris designers—Givenchy, Balenciaga, Chanel—which *Women's Wear Daily* began tracking ever more closely, and she was accused of being extravagant and unpatriotic in her selections. Her response to reports that she spent $30,000 a year on clothes did little to diffuse the air of scandal: "I couldn't spend that much unless I wore sable underwear."

Jacqueline Bouvier Kennedy was not a warm, homely everywoman. But while some observers saw Jackie as stiff and reserved, others were captivated by her mystique, her star quality. Jack Kennedy would often have cause to mutter to one of his aides, "Jackie's drawing more people than I am, as usual."

She carefully mediated her own image, as Larry O'Brien (who managed the Kennedy campaign) recalled: "She didn't think she should be seen smoking; I would hold a cigarette for her and she would take furtive puffs from time to time."

Jackie's accomplishments came in useful during 1959 and early 1960, as she crisscrossed the country with Jack on *Caroline,* the private jet Joe Kennedy had bought for $350,000. Her aptitude for languages enabled her to address different communities in their native tongue—a very popular touch. She spoke French in Eau Claire, Italian in Syracuse, and a few words of Polish in Milwaukee.

She found the constant glad-handing, speech-making, and being stared at very wearing. "You get so tired you catch yourself crying and laughing at the same time. But you pace yourself and you get through it," she commented. But she persisted with gusto when the mood took her. At one stage, Jack had to deal with other Senate business, so she covered Wisconsin alone, once memorably taking over a supermarket's public address system: "Just keep on with your shopping while I tell you about my husband … " Jack went on to win the Wisconsin Primary.

She had a very definite mind of her own. I think that's how she survived … by being very private and stubborn and saying no, and carving out her own existence

Laura Bergquist, journalist

By spring 1960, she was pregnant once more, and made few subsequent road trips ("Thank God I'm pregnant," she reportedly said. "I get to miss all those dreadful chicken dinners.") Joan Braden, who was at the same stage of pregnancy as Jackie and also working on the campaign, devised ways for her to keep supporting Jack from home. She wrote a syndicated "Campaign Wife" column, kick-started a conference-calling campaign, and appeared in TV advertisements, including one filmed with childcare guru Dr. Spock, aimed at pregnant women and young mothers. Against her doctor's advice, she attended the final Kennedy campaign meeting in New York City, touring the neighborhoods and taking part in a ticker-tape parade down Wall Street. She had reasoned: "If I don't go and Jack loses, I'll never forgive myself."

LOOK

NOW MORE THAN 6,300,000 CIRCULATION

20¢ OCTOBER 11, 1960

THE KENNEDY WOMEN

The females
of the family
are as formidable
as the men

MRS. JOHN F. KENNEDY

96

What amazed me the most
was the way people reacted to
Jackie. They identified with
the Princess. They had a wondrous
look in their eyes when they saw
her. After the dowdiness of Eleanor
Roosevelt, Bess Truman, and
Mamie Eisenhower, they were
looking for an aristocratic image.

Charles Peters, Democrat campaign organizer

Left: Jackie, representing the formidable Kennedy women on the cover of
LOOK magazine, October 20, 1960

Nothing disturbs me as much as interviewers and journalists. But if you make your living in public office, you're the property of every taxpaying citizen. Your whole life is an open book.

Right: Jackie serving coffee to reporters at the Kennedy's Georgetown home, September 1960

I wouldn't say that being married to a very busy politician is the easiest life to adjust to. The most important thing for a successful marriage is for a husband to do what he likes best and does well. The wife's satisfaction will follow.

Left: Jackie, Caroline, and Jack spending their last weekend together at Hyannis Port, Massachusetts, before he set off on the final leg of his presidential campaign, August 28, 1960

Her glamour and her unconventional beauty attracted attention and enticed the news media, for whom the couple had become a symbol of youth and vitality—a new symbol for a New Age. They looked more like movie stars than most movie stars.

Joseph Cerrell, Democratic Party campaigner

Right: **An autographed photo of Jackie, Jack, and Caroline, August 1960**
The appealing good looks of the First-Family-in-waiting could not help but win public favor. As one Cape Cod reporter said of Jackie: "It would be unendurable—indeed actually impossible—to write anything uncomplimentary about anyone with such eyes."

On the whole, she was a refreshing change from the usual candidate's wife because she did not bother to put on a phony show of enthusiasm about everything she saw and every local politician who she met. The crowds sensed that and it impressed them. When Jackie traveled with the Kennedy bandwagon, the crowds were twice as big.

Kenny O'Donnell, Kennedy aide

Left: Jack and Jackie greeting supporters in Hyannis Port, Massachusetts, July 17, 1960

She did have her views behind-the-scenes. She had a very strong protective instinct toward her husband, with a clear and correct idea of what his proper image should be.

Joan Braden

Left: **Jackie, beaming as she reads of her husband's first ballot victory for the Democratic presidential nomination, July 14, 1960**
She was forbidden by her doctor, John Walsh, to attend the Democratic Convention in New York, so ended up watching reports coming through on a rented television set with Caroline and her nanny.

She breathes all the political gases that flow around us, but she never seems to inhale them.

Jack

Jackie herself voted by absentee ballot—and cast a single vote, for Jack. "It's a rare thing to be able to vote for one's husband as president of the United States, and I didn't want to dilute it by voting for anyone else," she said, much to the consternation of other Democrats who would have appreciated her support.

I'm in a very intensive struggle.
What she does, or does not do,
really affects that struggle.
She is simply invaluable.

Jack

Left: Jack Kennedy applauds Jackie at a Democratic fund-raising dinner in Washington D.C. at which Senator Kennedy made his first nation-wide television speech, 20 September 1960

Next page: Jackie, pregnant and telegenic, talking to Dave Garroway on NBC'S *Today Show*, in one of her last pre-election interviews, broadcast September 14, 1960

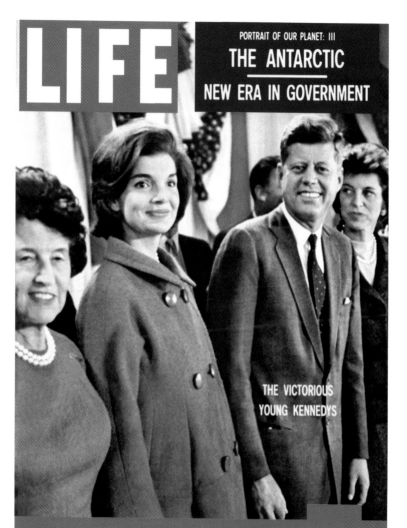

LIFE

PORTRAIT OF OUR PLANET: III

THE ANTARCTIC

NEW ERA IN GOVERNMENT

THE VICTORIOUS
YOUNG KENNEDYS

NOVEMBER 21, 1960

Hard-hearted Jack with tears in his eyes and his voice; the very first time I have seen the slightest display of emotion in the candidate and his team

Mary McGrory, journalist

Left: **"The Victorious Young Kennedys."** *LIFE* **magazine captured Jack's acceptance speech at Hyannis Port on November 9, 1960**

Next page: **The Kennedy clan at Hyannis Port after news of Jack's election win, November 9, 1960**

Jackie called the night of November 8, before the result was declared, "the longest night in history." Seated (left to right) are: Jack's sister Eunice (Mrs. R. Sargent Shriver); his parents Mr. and Mrs Joseph P. Kennedy; Jackie; his brother Edward Kennedy. Standing (left to right) are: his sister-in-law Ethel (Mrs. Robert F. Kennedy); his brother-in-law Stephen Smith; his sister Jean (Mrs. Stephen Smith); Jack; his brother Robert; his sister Patricia (Mrs. Peter Lawford); his brother-in-law R. Sargent Shriver; his sister-in-law Joan, Mrs. Edward Kennedy, and his brother-in-law Peter Lawford.

My wife and I look forward to a new administration and a new baby

Jack, in his acceptance speech

Right: **Jackie holding John Fitzgerald Kennedy Jr., at his christening on December 8, 1960**
President Elect Jack had just reached Palm Beach for a postelection vacation when he immediately had to fly back to see his wife and his new son.

A first lady of vision—1961 to 1963

Following the birth of John F Kennedy Jr. (known as John John), Jackie suffered from postnatal exhaustion and depression. But from her hospital bed in Georgetown, and then while she convalesced at the Kennedy home in Palm Beach, she furiously made plans for her new life as the president's wife. She appointed Letitia Baldridge to be her right hand woman as social secretary, and designer Oleg Cassini to produce her clothes.

Her most pressing project was the restoration of the tatty, unprepossessing White House interior into something resembling glory. She said to chief usher J. B. West: "We've got a lot of work ahead. I want to make this into a grand house!"

The thirty-one-year-old Jackie did not purely overhaul the appearance of the White House, she (along with Jack) transformed its incumbent atmosphere. First, the "dreary old Maison Blanche," as she called it, had to become a family home for the Kennedys. Caroline and John were a highly visible and audible part of the First Family around the corridors and offices of the White House. They went to nursery and school there, and played within sight of the Oval Office.

Jackie also established the White House as the site of a pleasurable social scene—a few times each week she would hold small-scale dinners with two or three other carefully chosen couples (there were certain jealousies between the closest members of the Kennedy inner circle). She would decide whether to invite guests over earlier the same day, having gauged Jack's mood. The ambience was so informal at these dinners that their friend Bill Walton renamed the White House, "the pizza palace on Pennsylvania Avenue." Every ten days, Jackie would give more elaborate dinner parties, assembling interesting combinations of guests—diplomats, intellectuals, reporters, and entertainers. She was at pains to keep the mood convivial, and deliberately joked about serious topics when Jack was supposed to be relaxing. British ambassador to Washington, David Ormsby-Gore, remembered that once when Jack started grumbling about air pollution, Jackie responded: "Why don't you just order the navy to spray our industrial centers with Chanel No 5?"

The larger dinner dances held in honor of various visitors to Washington became events to remember and mythologize. The tightfistedness of White House budgets was disregarded, and the Kennedys would serve free-flowing alcohol and delicious food by Jackie's French chef, René Verdon. Arthur Schlesinger said of the first such occasion on March 15, 1961, honoring Lee and her second husband Prince Stas Radziwill: "Never had girls been so pretty, tunes so melodious, an evening so blithe and unconstrained."

Jackie employed these social powers to fulfill her ambition to bolster the importance of the arts in American life. She filled her dinner table with artists and would invite performers to provide highbrow after-dinner entertainment. The writer Thornton Wilder commented: "She introduced for the artist a whole new world of surprised self-respect." Norman Mailer was frustrated that her choice of guests was not more adventurous: "One would offer her one's sword when Henry Miller was asked to the White House as often as Robert Frost and … good Gregory Corso could do an Indian dance in the East Room with Archibald McLeish." But Jackie pulled off a number of impressive coups including securing the cellist Pablo Casals to play a recital on November 13, 1961; he had previously pledged not to perform in the USA because of the country's support for Franco during the Spanish Civil War.

Jackie preferred to create her own brief and routine, rather than fulfill the countless official public engagements of the First Lady. She appeared to rapturous reception on a number of high-profile state visits overseas during 1961 and 1962, but, when it came to less glamorous duties, Jackie would often refuse to turn up, leaving Letitia Baldridge to find a stand-in (either the vice president's wife, Lady Bird Johnson, or one of the ever-eager Kennedy women). Jackie would escape the White House, with its lack of privacy, as frequently as possible—"You sit in a room and try to write a letter and someone comes in"—heading to the seclusion of their country home, Glen Ora, in rural Virginia, where she could spend time with her children and ride in the hunt. Every summer, she would leave Washington for several months, spending time at various Kennedy homes and Hammersmith Farm, and going on exotic holidays with her sister Lee and her jet-set friends.

Jackie's relentless globe-trotting led one newscaster to coin a joke, signing off each bulletin with: "Goodnight, Jackie. Wherever you are." Jackie defended herself to a friend: "The White House is such an artificial environment. It's a snake pit. If I don't take care of myself, I'll go mad."

Her sanity must have been tested by Jack's numerous extramarital affairs, which he pursued during her frequent absences from the White House. His most legendary was with Marilyn Monroe, but he also had liaisons with a gamut of women in their circle and on the staff—Mary Meyer; Diana de Vegh; Helen Chavchavadze; Jackie's press secretary, Pamela Turnure; and White House office girls Priscilla Wear and Jill Cowan, nicknamed Fiddle and Faddle. Pamela Harlech, a witty New York socialite, commented: "It was chic-er not to have slept with the president than to have slept with him."

Whether or not Jackie was aware of the exceptionally prolific nature of his fornication, in public she somehow maintained a defiant confidence in his love for her—at dinner dances she would take control by placing the most beautiful and intelligent women next to him. Journalist Hugh Sidey perceived that the Kennedys' "nomadic lives, their separateness—a phenomenon of great wealth—was not fully understood by the public, which clung to its older ideas of married life."

It was a relief for Jackie, in April 1963, to announce her pregnancy, which gave her legitimate cause to withdraw from the public gaze. However, in August she went into labor prematurely and when she gave birth to Patrick Bouvier Kennedy, he was afflicted with a respiratory ailment. He survived only two days. Unlike previous occasions when Jackie's problems giving birth had increased the distance between her and her husband, Jack and Jackie were bound together by the wretchedness of shared grief.

To try to help Jackie relax, Jack even allowed her to accept an invitation to spend time on the billionaire Aristotle Onassis' yacht, *Christina*—Onassis was at that point having an affair with Jackie's sister Lee Radziwill. Jack Kennedy was risking political damage, as Aristotle Onassis had a bad track record with the US government .

Later that fall, Jackie pledged to return to public life, and despite her antipathy to campaigning, planned to be at Jack's side as he worked to win a second term in office. She agreed to start by joining him on a challenging campaign trip to Texas. On November 22, as the president and his wife traveled in an open-top Lincoln car through the streets of Dallas, gunshots rang out. Two shots hit Jack Kennedy, the second shattering his skull.

"I just remember falling on him and saying, 'Oh, no, no, no,' … 'Oh, my God, they have shot my husband.' And 'I love you, Jack.' "

Turn on the lights so that they can see Jackie

Jack in the limousine on the way to the inauguration gala

Left: **Jackie and Frank Sinatra arriving at the preinauguration gala, at the National Guard Armory Washington D.C., January 19, 1961**

The event was organized by Sinatra and Peter Lawford as a glitzy, $100-a-head Democrat fundraiser, with a bill of celebrity performers including Harry Belafonte, Laurence Olivier, and Bette Davis. Sinatra sang "That Old Jack Magic." Jackie wore an exceptionally regal white satin gown designed by her newly appointed official couturier, Oleg Cassini, with a rosette at the waist—an eighteenth-century French touch. Her emerald and diamond jewelry was lent by Tiffany.

I was so proud of Jack, but I could scarcely embrace him in front of all those people, so I remember I just put my hand on his cheek and said, "Jack you were so wonderful." And he was smiling in the most touching and most vulnerable way. He looked so happy.

Above: **Jackie and Jack, Inauguration Day, January 20, 1961**
Jack Kennedy had just left the inaugural stand having sworn the presidential oath. His inauguration address, delivered following the poet Robert Frost's recitation of his work "The Gift Outright," was much admired. The *New York Times* called it, "a revival of the beauty of the English language."

I just crumpled. All my strength was finally gone, so I went home and Jack went on with the others.

Left: **Jackie and Jack, with Vice President Lyndon Baines Johnson, at the first inaugural ball in the Mayflower Hotel, January 20, 1961**
Her ivory georgette and silk gown was designed with the assistance of Diana Vreeland from *Harper's Bazaar*. She was still exhausted after the birth of John Kennedy Jr. and despite the help of a brown Dexedrine pill, only made it to two out of a string of five inaugural balls.

Interview with Oleg Cassini
OFFICIAL COUTURIER TO JACQUELINE KENNEDY
New York, December 2004

Oleg Cassini was a naturalized White Russian aristocrat and brother of social commentator Igor Cassini, who had named Jackie "Debutante of the Year" in 1947. A socialite friend of Joe Kennedy and a dress designer, Cassini had started his career designing costumes for Hollywood films. He had been married to actress Gene Tierney and engaged to Grace Kelly. Jackie appointed him to provide her wardrobe in December 1960, and he produced over three hundred outfits for her during the Kennedy administration.

I had first met her in the early fifties. I thought she was a very charming, well-educated young lady. We moved in the same circles and I had a chance to talk with her and dance with her. I thought that she was full of life, an optimist. She could also be very difficult. If you had disappointed her for some reason or another, you could be at a party seated next to her and she would be cool toward you.

I did not consider her a serious fashion person at that time, but she had a good figure for clothing. The remarkable thing was that she selected me in the first place. When she was in hospital recuperating from the birth of John John, I heard from her secretary, who said Mrs. Kennedy would like you to bring in some of your work. I was in Nassau at the time, so I took a plane to New York and made some sketches I thought she might like. What I was looking for was to design a silhouette that was just her silhouette—the sketches I took along, I made them look like her.

When I went to see her, all around her she had sketches from all these different designers. She asked me if I wanted to design

something for her, and I looked around and said, 'Not really. If you have two or three designers it will be war, you will go from one battle to another and spend your whole life in fittings.' I told her she should pick one person, and she started laughing and said, 'Then it's going to be you.'

I had a European background, which she always wanted in her designs, but I had become a naturalized American after my wartime service—her designer had to be an American for political reasons.

Above: **Jackie dancing with Oleg Cassini at the Belmont ball in Palm Beach, Florida, June 1954**
Jackie had known the well-connected fashion designer Cassini since 1952, and he became her official couturier when she reached the White House.

Then there was my Hollywood background, the ability to get a script and create a personal wardrobe. With her, it was like working on a picture except with her as the star. I was trying to be an image-maker. To me, she looked mysterious—like one of the goddesses of Ancient Egypt. Her eyes were very wide apart, she had the square, broad shoulders very much like you see in Egyptian hieroglyphics. She had a long torso and wonderful posture. It combined to make a very fetching picture. The evening gown in Swiss double satin I designed for her to wear to the inauguration gala was one of her favorites. In it, she became the goddess. The little beige coat I designed for her to wear to the inauguration was also effective—it made her look extra youthful next to all the other women, who looked like bears in their fur coats.

My whole career hinged on the way people would react the first time she was photographed in my clothes, and it was a big success. If I had done a poor job or if she had not been happy, I would have been out. While she was in the White House, I had a workroom with eight very good seamstresses dedicated to Jackie's wardrobe. It was a very demanding job, as her plans would change frequently. I would have to study the weather in every place she was going and change my designs when her plans changed. I kept designing my own line, but it did not include any of the same clothes that I designed for her.

I think Jack was just as surprised as anyone else by the transformation of his wife. He realized quickly that she was a first-class ambassador. She became a political plus to him; the world paid her homage wherever she went. There was a different kind of relationship than you would expect from a dress designer and their employer. I was a friend of the president and I would go to Washington not only for fittings, but also as a guest at their parties. I spent more weekends with them than I did with anyone.

I had many enemies at the time trying to minimize the work I was doing, because suddenly it propelled me into the list of the great designers of the world. *Womenswear Daily* started a whole campaign sniping at me, but I had to accept it, and just go on trying to make more and more attractive clothes for her.

People were saying that she suddenly became a genius, who had all the ideas for her fantastic clothes. She might say to me that she had seen a portrait of Catherine the Great wearing a wonderful ribbon or something, so we would look at ribbons together.

But generally, there was no time for that stuff. She would say, 'Oleg, I'm going to India … do you think pink would be a good color? Maybe orange?'

It was never a confrontational relationship. She would never have worn anything she did not like, so I assume she liked all the clothes of mine that she wore.

TWENTY-FIVE CENTS

JANUARY 20, 1961

TIME

THE WEEKLY NEWSMAGAZINE

JACQUELINE
KENNEDY

$7.00 A YEAR

VOL. LXXVII NO. 4

Her social graces masked tremendous awareness, an all-seeing eye, ruthless judgment, and a steely purpose

Arthur Schlesinger

Left: **A portrait of Jackie, the new First Lady, by Boris Chaliopin on the cover of *TIME* magazine, January 20, 1961**

I think the major role of the president's wife is to take care of the president and his children

Above: **Jackie with Jack, Caroline, and John Jr. on the cover of** *LOOK***, January 20, 1961**

Right: **Jackie and the family entering the White House, February 4, 1961**
Jackie and Jack were reunited with Caroline and John, who had been looked after by their nanny Maud Shaw and nurse Luella Hennessy in Joe Kennedy's home in Palm Beach during the inauguration events.

I do not consider myself part of the hunt country life. I appreciate the way people there let me alone.

Left: **Jackie at the Piedmont Hunt, March 26, 1961**

Jackie and the children would spend from Thursday to Monday at Glen Ora, their 400-acre retreat in Middleburg, Virginia, most weeks. She saw it as a place of privacy where she would ride regularly with the Piedmont and Orange County hunts.

The Jackie look

Jacqueline Kennedy's wardrobe had been making unprecedented numbers of headlines all the way to the White House. She quickly realized that, with the insatiable interest in every seam and hemline, her sartorial decisions were political as well as esthetic.

Her taste was for "terribly simple, covered-up clothes," as she wrote in 1960 to the editor of *Harper's Bazaar*, Diana Vreeland, when asking for her fashion advice. Georgetown dressmaker Mimi Rhea, who made clothes for Jackie when she first worked in Washington, recalls that Jackie "had a perfect horror of overdressing."

As a senator's wife, Jackie had been ordering her clothes from Paris couture houses, principally Givenchy, as well as Bugnand and Chanel, or alternatively obtaining copies of her favorite Paris designs from Bergdorf Goodman or Ohrbach.

However, it was imperative that as First Lady she should support the American garment industry—Mamie Eisenhower's wardrobe consisted of the proper yet decorative designs of Mollie Parnis. Soon after Jack was elected and she had given birth to John Jr., she requested sketches from various promising American designers—Norman Norell, Stella Sloat, Ben Zuckerman—from her hospital bed in Georgetown. While convalescing, she decided to appoint Oleg Cassini, a friend since the 1950s and a one-time Hollywood costume designer, as her official couturier. All Cassini's bills were to be sent to Joe Kennedy to avoid negative publicity.

The choice of Cassini surprised John Fairchild, the editor of *Womenswear Daily* and a keen Jackie-watcher, who noted: "None of the fashion intellectuals had considered him an important designer." But in Cassini, Jackie had made an astute selection. Not only did he possess the skill and taste to design a personalized wardrobe for Jackie, he was also cooperative and willing to tolerate her various provisos. She was able to declare him as her designer, but would still continue buying from French houses through Lee and various friends, while he acted as an effective fashion "beard." She briefed him in an extensive letter on December 13, 1960:

"One reason I am so happy to be working with you is that I have some control over my fashion publicity which has got so vulgarly out of hand … I refuse … to be the Marie Antoinette or Joséphine of the 1960s." She added: "Just make sure no one has exactly the same dress I do—I want all mine to be original and no fat little women all hopping around in the same dress."

Both Cassini and Jackie had a keen idea of the overall impression each outfit would create in the context in which she would be appearing. At the White House performance by cellist Pablo Casals, Jackie, in a chartreuse beaded Cassini gown, was described as "a willowy medieval princess who had stepped down from a painting."

Jackie's glossy leonine hairstyle would be straightened and coiffed for important occasions by New York hairdresser, Kenneth Battelle, known simply as Kenneth. She disliked hats ("I feel absurd in them") and settled on pillboxes (a style which had been available for several years) or berets, because they could sit on the back of her head and not flatten her hair. Bergdorf Goodman's saleswoman, Marita O'Connor, sourced shoes for Jackie, who was ever-conscious of her large feet. One memo Jackie fired off read: "Please order me a pair of alligator shoes size 10A—pointed toe but not exaggerated—no tricky vamp business" … Despite the understated, refined nature of Jackie's look—an A-line silhouette with unfussy accessories—it proved to be a popular hit.

Her garments began to be copied extensively by mass-market manufacturers; as First Lady Betty Ford noted: "It was epidemic, that wardrobe." Her appeal was such that shop mannequins were designed in her image. Jackie had barely been First Lady for two months when the phrase "the Jackie look" became a recognized part of the marketing lexicon, although she persisted in vain attempts to prevent it being so.

Although she headed the New York Couture Group's Best Dressed List for four consecutive years from 1961, and costume designer Edith Head deemed her "the greatest single influence in history," Jackie had her critics. Designer John Moore dismissed her clothes as "ill-fitting," and her skirts as "too short." In August 1961, she was subjected to a stinging attack from reporter Beatrice Vincent, who criticized her church clothes: "A skimpy, sleeveless shift is incorrect for church. So are bare toes peeking out of sandals; so is a kerchief knotted untidily under the chin."

Jackie did not dress with the intention of blazing a trail. Her priorities—beauty, taste, and dignity—were the same she applied to every other aspect of her life as First Lady. Hamish Bowles, the fashion writer and historian who curated the major retrospective of her White House wardrobe, defined the ruling element of her style as "a reductive elegance that ensured her clothing would remain a quiet foil to her personality."

Right: **Jackie, having cut a ribbon to officially open the annual Washington Cathedral flower market, May 5, 1961**
As time progressed, it became more difficult for her social secretary Letitia Baldridge to get her to appear at engagements such as this.

Jackie's style ... helped to break down a certain puritanism that had always existed in America and which insisted it was wrong to wear jewelry, wrong to wear fancy hairdos, wrong to live elegantly and graciously, wrong to wear tailored clothes

Hebe Dorsey, fashion critic

Left: Jackie in her official White House portrait taken by Mark Shaw, May, 1961

Next page: Jackie, the epitome of sporty chic relaxing with her mother and stepfather aboard the US Coast Guard Yacht *Manitou*, Narraganset Bay, September 9, 1962

International First Lady

Jackie's potency on the international stage astounded everyone, including herself. The celebrity allure which had first showed its worth on the presidential campaign trail was now enormously magnified by her status as First Lady.

The moment of realization came when Jackie and the president arrived in Paris on May 31, 1961. Half a million people lined the streets and left the president in no doubt as to who they had principally come to see, with their screams of "Jack-eee! Jack-eee!" Jack was forced to comment wryly to the French press: "I do not think it entirely inappropriate for me to introduce myself. I am the man who accompanied Jacqueline Kennedy to Paris."

Francophone Jackie, with her adoration of and comprehensive knowledge of French culture, found herself in her element. Over lunch with General de Gaulle in the Élysée Palace, Jackie was able to keep his rapt attention, conversing in her "low, slow French" about various figures in French history, from Louis XVI to the Duc d'Angoulême. She was entranced by the opportunity to dine later that day in the Hall of Mirrors at the Palace of Versailles, and de Gaulle was entranced in return by this "charming and ravishing woman with extraordinary hair and eyes" dressed in a Givenchy gown of ivory embroidered silk.

Jack was exceptionally proud of his wife, whose wit and chic had been saluted both by the French public and their political leaders. His aide, Kenny O'Donnell, points out: "Privately, he gave Jackie credit for establishing an easy and intimate understanding between himself and de Gaulle … She drew the fascinated French President into long and entertaining conversations with her husband that probably made him more relaxed with Kennedy than he had ever been with another head of a foreign government." Jackie clearly relished playing a pivotal role at her husband's side. "I think that's when she really began enjoying it all. Up to that point, she was just his wife … Afterward, she realized she had great influence on people," said Jean Kennedy Smith, her sister-in-law.

In one notable instance Jackie, somewhat reluctantly, represented America without Jack on what was termed a "semiofficial" two-week tour of India and Pakistan in March 1962. (It quickly escalated to the magnitude of a state visit.) It was a calculated move. The Indian prime minister, Nehru, had previously visited the president and Jackie at Hammersmith Farm in November 1961, and was, according to J. K. Galbraith, American ambassador to India, "deeply in love" with Jackie, whilst being unresponsive and monosyllabic with Jack.

Jackie went, accompanied by her sister Lee, on the thrice-postponed tour and enthusiastically experienced Indian customs and culture—she rode with Lee on an elephant and stood on her head when Nehru attempted to introduce her to yoga.

"Jackie's effect on the Indians was just wonderful," remembers Galbraith. "Nehru was by all odds the strongest figure in India and he was captured by Jacqueline Kennedy."

Jackie's background preparations (including studying Linguaphone tapes to improve her Spanish before a visit to Mexico) were of immense symbolic value, and proved to be politically invaluable. She had a gift for foreign languages that was highly unusual at that time in America. The combination of her dazzling looks and her wish to communicate with people in their own tongue won her overwhelming adulation.

She was intensely interested in foreign affairs. The president ... realized she could do a big job for him

Letitia Baldridge

Right: **Jackie on her first state visit to Ottawa, Canada, May 16, 1961**
The turnout for Jack and Jackie was bigger than had come to see Queen Elizabeth, with a quarter of Ottawa's 280,000 population estimated to have lined the streets, many calling out, "Jackie! Jackie!"

Jackie, in her cleverly selected red Pierre Cardin suit, was full of admiration for the Royal Canadian Mounted Police's equestrian drills. And she scored "a major triumph" with Canada's normally restrained citizens and statesmen.

In addition to her ancestry and her passion for French culture and history, Jackie had a long-held admiration for de Gaulle himself—during World War II, she had named her poodle "Gaullie" and, later, she avidly read de Gaulle's memoirs while accompanying Jack on the campaign trail. On their visit to Paris, her influence served to help Kennedy to better understand France, while her faultless chic wowed the 500,000-strong crowds.

TIME magazine noted: "Thanks in a large part to Jackie Kennedy at her prettiest, Kennedy charmed the old soldier into unprecedented flattering toasts and warm gestures of friendship." For Jackie, the trip was bliss, and not only because of the attention and admiration lavished upon her. She bonded with the French culture minister, André Malraux—the novelist and ex-Resistance fighter—who showed her round the collections at the Jeu de Paume gallery and took her to Malmaison, residence of Empress Joséphine. She attended the final gala dinner in the Hall of Mirrors at the Palace of Versailles in a Givenchy gown and watched the Paris Opéra Ballet perform in the restored Louis XV theater, reporting breathlessly: "I thought I was in heaven. I have never seen anything like it."

She played the game very intelligently. Without mixing in politics, she gave her husband the prestige of a Maecenas

Charles De Gaulle

Left: **Jackie resplendent in a Givenchy gown, with President Charles de Gaulle at the Palace of Versailles during the Kennedys' official visit to France, June 1, 1961**

Kennedy's wife ... was youthful, energetic, and pleasant. She knew how to make jokes and was ... quick with her tongue. She had no trouble finding the right word to cut you short if you weren't careful with her.

Nikita Khruschev

Right: **Jackie conversing with the Soviet premier, Nikita Khruschev, at the Schönbrunn Palace, Vienna. June 3, 1961**
During the banquet, Jackie was coquettish in her behavior with Khruschev, who admired her "exquisite" shimmering pink-silver gown while she laughed heartily at his jokes—she commented he was "almost cozy."

De Gaulle told the president and Mrs. Kennedy that ... it was Nina Khruschev who must be observed, for she reported back everything to (her husband). In Vienna, Jackie put all of her attention on Mrs. Khruschev, making a good impression on her, which might, in turn, help the diplomatic freeze ... between the two superpowers.

Jamie Auchincloss

Left: Jackie with Mrs. Nina Khruschev at Palais Pallavicini, Vienna, June 4, 1961

The Queen was pretty heavy going

Right: **Jackie, as a dinner guest of Queen Elizabeth and Prince Phillip at Buckingham Palace, London, June 5, 1961**

The Kennedys had a brief stay in London with Lee and her second husband, Prince Stas Radziwill. They were invited to dinner at Buckingham Palace. There was a question as to whether Lee and Stas, who were both divorced, could be invited to the palace. The Queen was persuaded to invite them, but Jackie joked that she got her revenge by also inviting "every Commonwealth minister of agriculture they could find."

Nest page: **Reception by the Japanese prime minister, Hayato Ikeda, Washington D.C., June 21, 1961**

Vice President Lyndon Johnson and his wife Lady Bird also attended. Lady Bird was an all-purpose understudy for Jackie in her official duties, —called upon so often that she was dubbed "Saint Bird" in the East Wing.

She stands for ... foreign languages and an effort to understand foreign people in a country that tends to think it is the only country and that English is the only language

Charlotte Curtis

Left: **Jackie with Jack arriving in Bogotá, Colombia, on their Latin America tour, December 17, 1961**

The president and his wife's four-day, whistle-stop trip to Puerto Rico, Colombia, and Venezuela was deemed by *TIME*, "more a schmaltzfest than a bold adventure." The warmth of the reception accorded Jackie was not always extended to Jack. In Venezuela, Communist students at the university in Caracas displayed a sign that read "KENNEDY—NO, JACQUELINE—YES." In Colombia, the message was "Yankee Go Home, Jackie Come Back."

A First Lady's warm embrace or cold stare or furrowed brow can affect her husband's mind and mood, and maybe even ultimately shake nations ... If anything, Jackie made light of her influence

David Ormsby-Gore, British ambassador to Washington

Left: Jackie being escorted by Jack to the Kennedy private plane, *Caroline,* as she sets off for her semiofficial tour of India and Pakistan, March 8, 1962

After pressure from cardinals favorable to the Kennedys, the Pope agreed ... to allow the reopening of Lee's case

Sarah Bradford

Right: **Jackie meeting Pope John XXIII, the Vatican, March 11, 1962**
Jackie, dressed dramatically and appropriately in a floor-length dress of black silk and wool, was granted a private audience with the Pope. The more expedient reason for her visit was to ask for an annulment for Lee's first marriage to Michael Canfield, so that she could marry the Catholic Prince Stas Radziwill in a religious ceremony—Lee's previous petition had been turned down. Later that year, Lee's first marriage was annulled.

Nehru was greatly attracted by Jackie, and this led to a more amiable view of the US without much doubt

J. K. Galbraith, American ambassador to India

Above: **Jackie with Prime Minister Nehru's daughter, Indira Gandhi, March 14, 1962**

Indira taught Jackie the *namaste*—the traditional Indian greeting with hands pressed together. When Jackie repeated it to the crowds in Udaipur, they shouted in admiration: "Ameriki Rani!" ("Queen of America!")

Left: **Jackie with Prime Minister Nehru and his dog Maghu in the garden of Nehru's home in New Delhi, India, March 14, 1962**

Nothing else happened in India while Mrs. Kennedy was here. Her presence completely dominated the Indian scene.

Prew Bhatia, editor of *The Times of India*

Left: **Jackie in Udaipur, India, where she cruised on Lake Pichola, March 17, 1962**

On the nine-day tour of India, Jackie was introduced to sights of exceptional beauty, visiting the Taj Mahal by moonlight and sailing down the Ganges on a marigold-decorated boat.

Jackie's wardrobe, which featured dresses by Oleg Cassini and Gustave Tassell, was particularly noticeable due to the head-turning color choices—there was apricot, yellow, ice blue, bright pink, and lavender, all easily visible in a crowd or from a distance. Lee, also immaculately dressed by Cassini, acted as a companion and lady-in-waiting to Jackie on the trip.

Next page: **Jackie receiving traditional indian *tilak* (mark of auspiciousness) March 19, 1962**

During their two-day visit to Jaipur, Jackie and Lee stayed at the palace of the Maharana and Maharanee.

It feels unnatural to me to go on such a long semiofficial trip without my husband. I have missed my family and have no desire to be a public personality on my own.

Left: **Jackie and Lee riding a camel on the lawn of President Ayub Khan's residence, Karachi, March 25, 1962**

They spent five days as the guests of the president, who presented Jackie with a ten-year-old bay gelding named Sardar. She rode the hunter for fifteen minutes and pronounced him "perfect." The India and Pakistan trip involved nearly fifty schedule changes—partly in response to criticism in *Newsweek* that the tour had involved too many palaces and not enough hospitals and orphanages. The logistical challenges left Letitia Baldridge ill with exhaustion and she was flown back to London early to recover.

Interview with Letitia Baldridge

WHITE HOUSE SOCIAL SECRETARY AND
JACKIE'S CHIEF OF STAFF
Washington DC, December 2004

Letitia "Tish" Baldridge was the White House social secretary and Jacqueline Kennedy's chief of staff from the Kennedys' arrival at the White House until May 1963. Before working for Jackie, she had worked for ambassadors' wives Evangeline Bruce at the American embassy in Paris and Clare Boothe Luce in Rome. Baldridge was described as a "genius in joviality."

I had first met Jackie in Washington after the war, as our parents were friends. I had gone to parties that her family gave out at Merrywood; I was three years ahead of her at Farmington; and then when she was living in Paris, I was working there.

She was very mature even then, she had 'been around'—not in a sexual way, but in a social way. She knew how to handle herself in social situations with people who were much older than her, and had gained a lot of knowledge from being around older people.

She was pretty quiet, because everyone would come to her, like moths to a flame. She would not try to be immensely funny or loud; she would have quiet conversations with people one-on-one. Her reticence provided a mystery which was irresistible. Jackie always had that and used it to her advantage.

When she became First Lady, she grew up and matured. She suddenly showed her brains and became enormously sophisticated about politics; she knew all the accomplishments of the different heads of state. The president always took her seriously—it was a working relationship.

The Kennedys made a young and unstuffy White House. There were a lot of laughs. As I knew the protocol from my jobs at the embassies, nobody challenged me in my job, which was just marvelous.

Every morning Jackie and I would talk on the phone and I would see her in her residence once or twice a day. She could not finish our meetings quickly enough. To her, I meant work; I was a pain in her side. She was very professional about it.

Above: **Letitia Baldridge (right) accepting a matched pair of antique candy jars on behalf of Jackie, 1961**

I would put lots of questions to her, she would ask the president at nighttime and I always got the answer the next day. I would say: 'There's this chapter of women, they helped a great deal with the campaign, please, please receive them,' and she would say: 'I won't.'

So I would try and rearrange things. Lady Bird Johnson was a frequent substitution for Jackie, and it all worked. We had to be creative with excuses for Jackie—it was our duty. Sinus trouble was one. When she was pregnant, that gave us an excuse to get her out of everything. She gave and gave and then when she wanted to stop giving, she stopped. And everybody forgave her—she was so popular she could get away with anything.

Jackie transformed social occasions at the White House. The long tables with white damask cloths were replaced by cozy round tables with colored circular cloths. And she wanted all the great artists to be there, and the great educators from the major universities—that spiced up the guest lists. The Kennedys would bring a really exciting group—everyone would come up with suggestions. Of course, the West Wing would try and get all these politicians and contributors in, and then we would carefully subtract them from the list.

My office would plan the seating, although Jackie would seat the smaller private dinner parties herself. We had a staff of calligraphers who would do all the invitations and place cards.

In terms of spending on social occasions, we would do whatever we wanted and take the heat afterward. People were going to criticize any show of pomp and circumstance at the White House, but we knew we had to have pomp and circumstance. When the heat got too much, the president would react to public opinion and say, 'Cool it.' We would have much less expensive food and less expensive Californian wines.

I used to have to go on all of the state visits with Jackie. I used have to go ahead of them to do advance planning along with Pierre Salinger [Kennedy's press secretary] and McGeorge Bundy, head of the Secret Service. We would plot out every step they would make and every word the First Lady would speak. I would make sure all her requirements were met, that there was a hairdryer in her bathroom, that there was the special pillow she slept on. I produced pages of briefing papers which I tried to make amusing for her.

She would have such an effect on the important people she met. I would send her up notes saying, 'The minister was gaga for you.' After meeting them, she would imitate the heads of state, which the president loved—she did a fabulous Macmillan impersonation.

The trips could be hell for me, with schedules changing all the time. On the India and Pakistan trip, Jackie and Lee were troopers. I remember we all had tea at Prime Minister Nehru's house, with him and Indira Gandhi. Out came a big, beautiful basket and inside was a big cobra, and they brought out a mongoose and set them to fight. The cobra killed the mongoose. I could see Jackie swallowing hard— I knew she was sick in her stomach. Lee was looking away. But afterward, Jackie smiled a wide smile and said, 'That was wonderful, Mr. Prime Minister. How exciting, I'm so glad you showed us.' She said all the right things, even when she wanted to throw up.

Above: **Jackie alongside Jack in Mexico City, June 29, 1962**
TIME magazine wrote: "By the uncounted millions, Mexicans gave him
and his pretty wife ... the greatest outpouring of goodwill he had yet seen
on his travels."

Left: **Jackie, Mexico City, June 30, 1962**
She is distributing presents to children at the National Institute for the
Protection of Children.

Next page: **Jackie at the National Gallery of Art, Washington DC,
January 8, 1963**
At the gala unveiling of the *Mona Lisa* Jackie stands next to the French
minister of culture, André Malraux. Also present are Jack Kennedy, Mme
Malraux, and Vice President Lyndon Johnson.

Jackie wore so many masks she was impossible to decipher. With her elevation to the position of First Lady, she became ever more elusive, more secretive, more dramatic.

Charlotte Curtis, former dormitory mate at Vassar and journalist

Right: **Jackie and Jack wait at Union Station Washington D.C. for the arrival of King Hassan of Morocco, March 27, 1963**

The state dinner held for King Hassan was attended by Samuel Barber, Myrna Loy, Agnes de Mille, and Alan Jay Lerner, who were entertained by the New York City Light Opera Company. The monarch obviously enjoyed Jackie's company and a few years later attempted to give her a Moorish palace in Marrakesh.

Perhaps saving old buildings and having the new ones be right isn't the most important thing in the world—if you are waiting for the bomb—but I think we are always going to be waiting for the bomb. And it won't ever come.

Left: **The crowds in Berlin sending "Greetings to Jacqueline" on the occasion of President Kennedy's visit to the Berlin Wall, June 26, 1963** Jack had left the pregnant Jackie at Camp David to go to make his historic speech declaring his solidarity with the people of Berlin and his support for them against the Soviets. His language skills were not on a par with the absent Jackie (Lee accompanied the president instead) and he declared "Ich bin ein Berliner" rather than the more correct "Ich bin Berliner." In Jack's version he was declaring himself a type of local doughnut.

The making of a grand house

The restoration of the White House into a place of historical interest and integrity, as well as good taste, was to be Jackie's most concrete legacy as First Lady.

She realized the extent of what she called "my project" the day she left the hospital after having John Jr. and was given a tour by incumbent First Lady Mamie Eisenhower. Even in her weakened state (Mamie refused to offer Jackie a wheelchair unless she specifically requested it) she took in a bewildering number of details, her mind seething with the work that she saw needed to be done.

Jackie told her newly appointed social secretary, Letitia Baldridge, that the Eisenhower White House looked like "a hotel that had been decorated by a wholesale furniture store during a January clearance." One notable feature of the Eisenhowers' living quarters was a pair of adjacent portholes for built-in television sets so that Mamie and Ike could watch their preferred soap operas and westerns simultaneously while eating their dinner from trays. Jackie decried the "seasick green" curtains, the "Mamie pink on the walls," the Victorian mirrors, and the Oval Room, which put her in mind of the Soviet prison, the Lubianka.

Jackie's convalescence in Palm Beach was a frenzy of planning, as she made pages of notes in her lined yellow legal pads. J. B. West, chief usher at the White House, sent her annotated photos of each of the 132 rooms, and she borrowed helpful books and journals from the Library of Congress to garner more historical detail. Her original aim, which later became less focused, was to restore the White House to reflect the period when it was completed by President Jefferson in 1802.

As soon as the Kennedys moved into the unwelcoming White

House (the central heating system was hardly working and the fireplaces unused), Jackie set about her project with urgency. She said on arrival that she "felt like a moth banging on the windowpane. The windows hadn't been opened for years."

She sought the advice of society decorator Mrs. Henry Parish (known as Sister Parish), who had decorated her previous home on N Street in Washington. Jackie also enlisted the help of Rachel Lambert "Bunny" Mellon, a wealthy horticulturist friend whom she had looked up to as an arbiter of taste since meeting her when Caroline was a baby. (Deborah Duchess of Devonshire said of Bunny: "She lived in her own realm of beauty and perfection.")

A new atmosphere blew through the White House like a wind with a clearing sky. Cupboards and warehouses were opened to search for historic treasures.

Bunny Mellon

The three women quickly effected cosmetic changes—such as replacing the drooping palms in the state rooms with Mellon's relaxed flower arrangements inspired by seventeenth-century Dutch still life paintings—but Jackie's intentions became formalized with the creation of the White House Fine Arts Committee in late February, 1961, in order to track down the "authentic furnishings" required. Henry du Pont, the eighty-year-old authority on American furnishings, became its chairman.

One of the most active members of the Fine Arts committee was Jayne Wrightsman, who was the wife of oil billionaire Charles Wrightsman, and a Palm Beach neighbor of the Kennedys. She shared Jackie's deep passion for the opulent French decorative arts.

She was an also an avid and highly informed collector. As well as financing the decor for the Blue Room, Wrightsman was responsible for introducing Jackie to Stéphane Boudin, a Parisian interior designer who had worked in Buckingham Palace and Joséphine Bonaparte's Malmaison. So keen was Jackie to have his elegant expertise on the project that she invited Boudin for a four-day visit before the committee was set up. As he was not American, his involvement had to be kept secret—the more imaginative Washington gossips speculated he had been smuggled into the White House wrapped in a rug.

With Parish, du Pont, and Boudin all vying to make their mark on the White House, Jackie, assisted by Jayne Wrightsman, needed every ounce of her tact to keep them all on board—Parish nearly resigned a number of times, but Jackie appeased her with letters emphasizing her great value to the endeavor.

"Jackie's charm made everything work," recalled the Kennedys' journalist friend, Joe Alsop. She not only convinced Lyndon Johnson to allow a crystal chandelier to be transferred from the Senate to the White House; she reclaimed a number of the best Cézannes from the National Gallery, which had previously been willed to the White House. She succeeded in drawing scores of private donations of valuable pieces of furniture and paintings. On August 4, 1961, the *Daily Telegraph* commented:

"The grand rush to become a White House Donor is a new kind of gold rush. It is better any day than trying to keep up with the Joneses. You are made as a patriot and a man or woman of substance when you become a White House giver."

With her White House curator Lorraine Pearce, Jackie put together a guidebook to inform visitors about each room's history, and raise funds for continuing restoration.

While work was in progress, Jackie tried to conceal finer details from the press. But still, any gaffe was reported on upon gleefully— the donated Baltimore desk that turned out to be fake, the role of Frenchman Stéphane Boudin, and the escalating costs (for example, $28,000 on fabrics for the Red Room). Jackie did collaborate in judiciously chosen publicity—first, she told *LIFE* of her plans for their September 1 issue:

Everything in the White House must have a reason for being there. It would be sacrilege merely to redecorate it … It must be restored.

She also memorably took part in an hour-long television special for CBS, which was filmed in January, 1962. Jackie was interviewed by Charles Collingwood, moving through the state rooms, reeling off the dates and donors of notable furniture. Her performance was generally well received, although writer Norman Mailer, who described her later in an *Esquire* article as "like a starlet who is utterly without talent." She won an honorary Emmy award, although CBS' Blair Clark recalls: "We had to amplify her voice so people could understand what she was saying."

Jackie's ambitions to preserve historical integrity extended to areas outside the White House, and she became involved in a number of projects to preserve other nineteenth-century Washington treasures. She pushed forward the project to save the buildings of Lafayette Square, wanted to renovate Blair House (where foreign visitors stayed), and was set on revamping Pennsylvania Avenue, the road that links the Capitol to the White House, hoping to include an opera house.

Above: **Jackie supervises workmen moving furniture for restoration, August, 1961**

Right: **Jackie examines plans of the White House, while her first curator, Lorraine Pearce, talks on the phone, July 1961**

Jackie Kennedy put a little style into the White House, and into being First Lady of the land, and suddenly "good taste" became good taste. Before the Kennedys, "good taste" was never the point of modern America at all.

Diana Vreeland

Left: **Jackie with CBS correspondent Charles Collingwood in the White House State Dining Room, February 14, 1962**
He interviewed her for the special program *A Tour of the White House with Mrs. John F. Kennedy.*

About 46.5 million people tuned in for the program, seventy-five percent of the viewing audience. Afterward, Jackie was deluged with 6,300 fan letters. CBS producer Perry Wolff said: "She knew her stuff. She was a combination of sophistication and ingenuousness, almost childlike, and it was so winning."

There have been some great wives in the White House—like Abigail Adams and Dolly Madison—so great that you can't think of their husbands, presidents, without thinking of them. It looks as though we are having another one now.

Robert Frost

Right: **Jackie with poet Robert Frost in the East Room at the White House, at the dinner held in honor of American Nobel Prize winners, April 29, 1962**

In her sea-green Grecian jersey dress by Oleg Cassini, Jackie welcomed 175 guests including forty-nine Nobel Prize winners, to the White House. The *Washington Post* proclaimed it "one of the most stimulating parties ever." Jerome Robbins' company, Ballets USA, performed in sweatshirts and sneakers, and actor Frederic March read a chapter from an unpublished Ernest Hemingway novel provided by his widow, Mary.

I worked carefully on the guest list for the state dinner, wanting to include artists admired abroad, not only the traditional, established ones ... I hoped his (Malraux's) visit would call attention to the importance of the arts

200

Left: **Jackie with André Malraux, the French minister of culture, at a state dinner held at the White House in his honor, May 11, 1962**

Jackie had huge admiration for Malraux, the ex-Resistance fighter and writer. "He's a true Renaissance man," she said of him; Letitia Baldridge described him as her "intellectual crush."

Jackie, who that night wore a pink strapless silk gown by Dior, assembled 168 guests including Tennessee Williams, Saul Bellow, Elia Kazan, George Balanchine and Arthur Miller.

Next page: **Jackie with her predecessor, Mamie Eisenhower, at the White House, June 22, 1962**

The pair were meeting for a tea to discuss the fund-raising plans for a National Cultural Center, a project Jackie saw as essential. As President Eisenhower had signed the first legislation towards its establishment, Mamie was appointed co-chairperson of the fund-raising committee. She agreed with the proviso that she did "not care to serve in an honorary capacity subordinate to Mrs. Kennedy." Predictably, this proved impossible, and Mamie only attended this one meeting.

She has a great deal in common with top movie stars. She knows when to hold herself back, while everyone else you know gives too much of themselves at one time.

Richard Avedon, photographer

Right: **Jackie and Jack at a dinner for Grand Duchess Charlotte of Luxembourg, April 30, 1963**

For the occasion, Jackie persuaded Basil Rathbone to perform various readings, including the St. Crispin's Day speech from *Henry V*, one of Jack's favorite passages. The Grand Duchess was impressed by Jackie, who had that month announced she was pregnant again, describing her as "America's most potent weapon, Madame la Présidente."

A mother in the White House

For someone of her class, not to mention her position as First Lady, Jackie has been credited with being an unusually warm and hands-on mother to Caroline and John Jr. She had them call her "Mommy" and took her role as mother more seriously than any other obligation that was conferred upon her when Jack became president.

The nanny, Maud Shaw, was in charge of Caroline and John's daily care, but Jackie was determined not to be an aloof, invisible mother. "One could raise a child with one's left hand, but why let it be such a casual operation when the responsibility in bringing more to the child's world is the greatest joy for the parent?" she said.

The White House, dominated by working offices, could have been a place where children were decidedly unwelcome and out of place. However, Jackie set a different precedent in the Kennedy White House. For security reasons, Caroline could no longer go to her nursery group in Georgetown, so Jackie made the decision to set up a nursery group of ten pupils. Two teachers, Anne Mayfield and Jaclin Marlin, were employed, and the nursery was paid for as a cooperative, with the parents of all the children contributing. A well-equipped schoolroom was set up in the third floor solarium, with a blackboard, hundreds of books, and a sandbox. Jackie organized the acquisition of a pregnant rabbit for the class so that the children could watch a mother rabbit with her babies. Whenever there was an official ceremony taking place on the White House Lawn, it would form part of the day's activities—the children would watch it take place. The class also had their own secluded playground on the South Lawn with a swing, slide, and tree house.

Susan Wilson, one of the other mothers, who had been at Vassar with Jackie, recalls: "Jackie thought it would be more natural for Caroline, to demystify the place, to make it less cold and formidable, to have kids scampering in the long hallways."

Having the children around all the time also allowed Jack to be part of their daily routine. Caroline and John would be with him at breakfast time and see him before bed, but also, as the children's playground was near his West Wing office, Jack could go and sit on the bench there when he took a break during the day. If he heard them playing while he was in his office, he would clap three times and they would run in to see him.

Within the abnormal parameters of White House life, Jackie strove to create a rounded childhood for Caroline and John. "I don't want them to think they are 'official' children," she said to the chief usher, J. B. West. Mirroring her own East Hampton upbringing, she bought the children numerous pets. There were ponies—Macaroni and Tex—as well as guinea pigs, lambs, chicks in a hatchery, and dogs, Clipper and Charlie. Caroline also had hamsters, Debbie and Billie, one of whom escaped and was tracked down in the president's bathtub.

For Jackie, one major means of protecting Caroline and John was to strictly limit press access to them. Jack, conversely, was much more relaxed about such exposure, and knowing the political value of being captured as a family man, he would grant photo opportunities while Jackie was away from the White House—John John was snapped hiding under his father's desk in the Oval Office.

Whenever she was away, Jackie would frequently make statements saying how much she missed her children. When she was with them, the pleasure she would take in playing with them was palpable—"Let's go kiss the wind!" she'd say to Caroline.

I think it's hard enough to bring up children anyway, and everyone knows that limelight is the worst thing for them. They get conceited, or else they get hurt ... They need their mother's affection and guidance and long periods of time alone with her.

Previous page: **Jackie and family on their way to the Easter Sunday church service in Palm Beach, April 22, 1962**

Left: **Jackie with Empress Farah, wife of the Shah of Iran, April 12, 1962**
They are touring the White House grounds, with Caroline's pony, Macaroni. Jackie's press secretary, Pamela Turnure, stands behind them—she ensured that Jackie's relations with the press followed her rule: "minimum information given with maximum politeness."

Jackie was very quiet, very nice, gentle, and serene. She was cooking spaghetti for Caroline. She bought sandals in Capri. She was more simple, less sophisticated than when she was (being) First Lady. In Italy, she was only a tourist.

Benno Graziani

Previous page: **Jackie playing with John Jr., summer 1962**
One of the most intimate and captivating images of an adoring mother and her mischievous son, who simply can't resist playing with her pearls.

Right: **Jackie with Caroline during their summer holiday in Ravello, Italy, August 1962**
Despite the constant attention of the press and the Secret Service men present for their protection, Jackie and Caroline enjoyed to the full their almost month-long stay with Lee and Stas in the twelfth-century Villa Episcopio in Ravello.

Above: **Jackie and President Ayub Khan of Pakistan with Sardar, the gelding he had given her during her Pakistan trip, Washington, September 25, 1962**

Right: **Jackie with John on Sardar and Caroline astride Macaroni, riding at Glen Ora, near Middleburg, Virginia. November 19, 1962**

She was a remarkable mother, the way she spoke and engaged the children

Sue Wilson

Right: Jackie lights candles on Caroline's fifth birthday cake, November 27, 1962

She kept her family together in the White House regardless of the limelight that suddenly hits a president

Bess Truman

Left: **Christmas Day at the Kennedy home in Palm Beach, 1962**
The Kennedys are with the Radziwills and their children, and their dogs Clipper and Charlie.

I want my children to be brought up in more personal surroundings, not in the state rooms. I don't want them to be raised by nurses and Secret Service agents.

Right: **Jackie with Caroline in the White House schoolroom, May 24, 1963**
J. B. West recalls that Jackie was "so happy, so abandoned, so like a little girl who had never grown up." With her children, her sense of mischief could have free rein—on the Halloween of 1961, she took Caroline trick-or-treating with Jean Kennedy Smith and her son Will. With Caroline dressed up as a little witch, and Jackie incognito in her ghost costume with eyeholes, they knocked on the doors of unsuspecting friends and White House staff.

I know my husband was devoted to me. I know he was proud of me. It took a very long time for us to work everything out, but we did, and we were about to have a real life together.

Right: **Jackie sailing off Cape Cod, August 4, 1963**

This photograph was taken three days before she would go into labor prematurely. She smoked throughout all her pregnancies—the health risks were not known at that time.

I will be back next year.
I will have another child.

Left: **Jackie and Jack leave Otis Air Force Base Hospital, Massachusetts in the full gaze of the press, August 14, 1963**

Jackie had given birth prematurely to Patrick Bouvier Kennedy, weighing 4 lb. 1 oz., a week previously. He died on August 9 from cardiac arrest—he was suffering from the respiratory disorder hyaline membrane disease.

Jack and Jackie were very close after Patrick's death. She hung onto him and he held her in his arms—something nobody ever saw at any other time because they were very private people

Bill Walton

Right: **Jackie with Jack, Caroline, and John John at Squaw Island, their house at Hyannis Port, the day she left hospital, August 14, 1963**
Also with them are their dogs Clipper (right) and Wolf (with Caroline).
Wolf had been given to Jack by the people of Ireland on a recent visit.
John John is playing with the "pupniks." They were born to Pushinka,
another pet dog who was a gift from the Russian people.

Onassis was charming, interesting, humorous, but there was nothing going on between him and Jackie. Jackie may have flirted a little, but that was how she related to men.

Suzanne Roosevelt

Left: **Jackie on board Aristotle Onassis' 325-foot luxury yacht, *Christina*, October 1963**

Jackie is with Suzanne Roosevelt (left) and Franklin Roosevelt Jr. (right). After Patrick's death, Jackie accepted an invitation from Greek tycoon Aristotle Onassis to convalesce on his yacht. Onassis' business reputation was shady; moreover, he and Lee were having an affair—and this caused gossip. Franklin Roosevelt Jr. and his wife were sent by Jack as chaperones to diffuse any possible air of scandal. The cruising party sailed across the Aegean to Istanbul, stopping in Lesbos, Crete, Skorpios, Onassis' private island, and Smyrna, Onassis' birthplace, where he regaled Jackie with tales of his escape from the city when the Turkish army took over in 1922.

She had clearly "grown up a lot" in that year ... Some of the arrogance had gone: there was a new humility in its place. The moods were less shifting, the wit less biting, the flares of aggression dimmed and deeper ... She had never been happier.

Robin Douglas-Home

Right: **Jackie with her family at a performance of the Black Watch Royal Highland Regiment on the White House South Lawn, November 13, 1963** The other spectators watching the drills and Highland dancing were 1,700 children aged six to thirteen from childcare agencies in the Washington area. Jackie's appearance, with Caroline and John Jr. in their new blue winter coats, marked the resumption of her duties as First Lady after the death of her premature baby six weeks earlier than expected.

Last trip—November 1963

Jackie returned from her hedonistic Greek cruise feeling distinctly indebted to her husband. Although he had been strongly advised by his press secretary, Pierre Salinger, and Jackie's press secretary, Pam Turnure, against allowing Jackie to spend time on Onassis' yacht, he had not stood in her way. On the contrary, he said: "Well, I think it will be good for Jackie, and that's what counts." Jackie wrote him ten-page letters, telling him about her days and how she loved and missed him; and Jack telephoned her, filling her in on the negative press reports circulating of parties which lasted until dawn, as well as photographs which showed her sunbathing in her bikini.

So, now, when it came to helping with Jack's difficult political campaign in Texas, she was ready and willing to shoulder her side of the task in a renewed spirit of partnership. But Jack was not looking forward to the trip—he knew that the political climate in the state was poisonous and had told Pierre Salinger "I wish I weren't going to Texas."

If Jack had unconscious forebodings, his worst fears were to be realized. In one split second, America lost a leader and the First Lady was plunged into the long nightmare of being widowed in front of a shocked and horrified world.

Left: **Jackie and Jack at the Rice Hotel in Houston, Texas, where Jackie made a speech in Spanish to the League of United Latin American Citizens, November 21, 1963**

Three times that day in Texas, we were greeted with bouquets of [the] yellow rose of Texas. Only in Dallas, they gave me red roses. I remember thinking—how funny, red roses for me.

Right: **Jackie and Jack as they arrived at Love Field, the start of the motorcade route through Dallas, November 22, 1963**

Jack had known that Jackie's understated elegance and refined manner would stand out in Texas. When discussing her outfit for their day in Dallas, he commented: "There are going to be all these rich Republican women … wearing mink coats and diamond bracelets … Show these Texans what good taste really is." Jackie accordingly wore a pink Chanel suit trimmed in navy with a matching pink pillbox hat.

Above: **Jackie and Jack traveling with Governor John Connally and his wife Nellie in the presidential Lincoln, November 22, 1963**

Jack had insisted they did not use the bubble top on the car, saying, "No, that's semisatisfactory, if you're going out to see the people, then they should be able to see you." In the shimmering heat, Jackie kept on putting her sunglasses on, with Jack periodically telling her to take them off again.

Above: **Moments after Jack's assassination, November 22, 1963**
Jackie scrambles onto the back of the Lincoln while her Secret Service
agent Clint Hill frantically tries to reach the moving car. In the turmoil
of these last, desperate seconds, Jackie was in a blind panic, crawling
toward her protection officer who was behind her on the running board of
the follow up car.

I remembered thinking, "How can they ask her to do this?" and then there she was. She said "I will be ready in a moment," and she did it.

Pamela Turnure

Left: **Jackie on Air Force One, November 22, 1963**
She is being consoled by Lyndon Baines Johnson and Lady Bird Johnson moments after Johnson took the Oath of Office. In her pink suit, stained and spattered with her husband's blood and brain fragments Jackie stood as witness to the swearing in of the next President.

The first widow

In the minutes, hours, and days following her husband's assassination, Jackie Kennedy's every action was imbued with deep symbolic importance. Despite the enormity of the pain and shock, Jackie was keenly aware that her own anguish was secondary to her principal role in this tragic world event.

From the first moments onward, Jackie's strongest instinct was the protection of Jack's memory. Immediately after the shooting, she lay over his body on the seat of the car, "just like a drift of blossoms" as Lady Bird Johnson recalls, hiding his shattered head from the world. She would not let him be taken from the car into Parkland Hospital until Secret Serviceman Clint Hill had wrapped his jacket around the president's head.

While her private actions reflected the intensity of her distress (at Parkland Hospital she took off her wedding ring and put it on Jack's finger, only to ask for it to be retrieved later that day), in her public gestures, Jackie was sure-footed. She made a point of being present, her face blanked by grief, while Lyndon Johnson took the Oath of Office on Air Force One, sitting on the tarmac at Love Field, Texas. She refused to change her Chanel suit, which was stained with blood and had fragments of brain matter still adhering to it, stating, "No. Let them see what they've done."

When the plane landed at Andrews Air Force Base near Washington, she did not want to make a secret arrival with Jack's casket. On disembarking, she was greeted by Bobby, in full view of a 300-strong crowd of the public and press.

That night, during the eight-hour wait for the autopsy to be completed at Bethesda Naval Hospital in Washington, between compulsively repeating in graphic detail what she remembered of the shooting, Jackie was comforting others. Ethel Kennedy recalls: "She was so warm and loving to everyone." However, Kennedy friend Ben Bradlee saw her as "this totally doomed child … looking burned alive."

Jack's funeral was already foremost in Jackie's mind—she approached it with the awareness that she was planning a future historical event. She sent a message to the chief of protocol, Angier Biddle Duke, to obtain the exact details of Abraham Lincoln's funeral, which became a template for her and her brother-in-law, Sargent Shriver, who organized the logistics of the occasion. Jackie wanted the Black Watch Royal Highland Regiment to be part of the ceremony—Jack and Jackie had watched them perform just two weeks before. Letitia Baldridge located the regiment in Knoxville, Tennessee. She also requested cadets from the Military College of Ireland, whose drill had impressed Jack on his visit to Dublin.

Jackie argued for a closed casket, which was eventually agreed upon as the reconstruction work on Jack's face made him resemble a "wax dummy."

The ceremonies were characterized by both pomp and simplicity. The horse-drawn gun carriage bearing the coffin was trailed by a black, riderless gelding with boots reversed in its stirrups. (Coincidentally, its name was Black Jack, her father's nickname, although Jackie did not know this at the time.) The procession, which followed the eight blocks from the White House to St. Matthew's Cathedral, was led by Jackie holding the hands of her children, Teddy and Bobby Kennedy flanking her. Behind the immediate family, at Jackie's request, walked Lyndon Johnson and the international heads of state, defying security advice.

At the service, Mass cards were distributed which read: "Dear God, please take care of your servant John Fitzgerald Kennedy."

There was no formal eulogy, but Reverend Philip Hannan gave an eleven-minute address that included remarks and passages from Jack's speeches as well as Bible passages. Jackie chose Ecclesiastes 3:1–8 ("To everything there is a season, and a time for every purpose under heaven ...") over the "too obvious" Psalm 23. The mourners left the cathedral to the notes of "Hail to the Chief."

Jackie's friend Bunny Mellon arranged the flowers for the Capitol, the church, and the graveside. For the church, she assembled summery daisies, white chrysanthemums, and stephanotis. By the graveside at Arlington National Cemetery, Mellon's basket of white roses and flowers from the White House rose garden was the sole arrangement. Jackie instructed Mellon that all the tributes from the public should be placed "far, far from the grave."

The Arlington hillside site was chosen over the Kennedy family plot at Brookline, Massachusetts—Defense Chief Robert McNamara persuaded the Kennedy family and his aides that the spot, where Jack had once admired the view over Washington, was the most fitting resting place.

Left: **Jackie leaving the White House with Caroline and John Jr. to escort their father's coffin to the Rotunda at the Capitol, November 24, 1963**

Next page: **Jackie and Caroline kissing the flag draped over John F. Kennedy's coffin in the Rotunda at the Capitol, November 24, 1963**
Jack's body lay in state there until his funeral the following day, while 250,000 mourners filed past in tribute.

To add to the symbolism of the scene, Jackie decreed that his tomb should have an eternal flame, like the tomb of the unknown soldier at the Arc de Triomphe. "Jackie had a great sense of the dramatic. There were no wrong notes," said her mother, Janet.

Following the burial, Jackie had yet further duties to fulfill, first receiving at the White House the 220 representatives from 102 nations who had attended the funeral, proffering each her personal gratitude. Afterwards she held a birthday party for John Jr., whose third birthday was that day. At midnight, after an informal wake with family and close staff and friends watching the funeral on television, Jackie and Bobby drove to Arlington where she laid a bouquet of lily of the valley on top of the freshly turned soil.

Several days later, Jackie asked Janet and Teddy to retrieve the caskets of baby Patrick and her stillborn baby Arabella from Brookline and take them to Arlington, where they were buried alongside their father on December 4.

The funeral and burial arrangements were just the beginning of Jackie's efforts to render Jack's legacy permanent. She requested that Lyndon Johnson rename Cape Canaveral Space Center in Florida as Cape Kennedy—which he did on November 29. (Jackie later regretted this, saying, "If I'd known Cape Canaveral was the name from the time of Columbus, it would have been the last thing Jack would have wanted.") Jackie also arranged for a plaque to be erected by the fireplace in the Lincoln Bedroom.

Right: **John Jr. stepping forward to salute his father at the funeral, November 25, 1963. Standing either side of Jackie are Teddy and Bobby Kennedy, with Peter and Pat Lawford behind them**

This plaque was to commemorate the Kennedy's time in the White House, before she moved out with her family to Governor Harriman's Georgetown house on December 6.

"She took the man she loved and made him unforgettable," Washington diarist Katie Louchheim observed. A week after the assassination, Jackie invited *LIFE* reporter Teddy White to Hyannis Port, where she had gone to tell her account of Jack's death to Joe Kennedy. She spoke with White for nearly four hours, during which she recounted to him how much Jack loved the song "Camelot" from Alan Jay Lerner's musical. She quoted the lyric to him:

"Don't let it be forgot, that once there was a spot, for one brief shining moment that was known as Camelot."

This vision of the Kennedy administration as Camelot, "a magic moment in American history when gallant men danced with beautiful women," was Jackie's romanticization, but it was one that Teddy White was prepared to let stand for posterity.

"All she wanted was for me to hang this *LIFE* epilogue on the Camelot conceit. So I said to myself … if that's all she wants, let her have it."

Left: **Left: Jackie holds the folded American flag that had covered Jack's coffin, after his burial at Arlington National Cemetery, Virginia, November 25, 1963**

There's only one thing I can do in life now—save my children. They've got to grow up without thinking back at their father's murder. They've got to grow up intelligently, attuned to life in a very important way. And that's the way I want to live my life too.

Right: **Jackie and Caroline arriving at 3036 N Street in Georgetown from the White House, December 6, 1963, escorted by her Secret Service agent Clint Hill**

This was the house of Governor Averell Harriman, a friend of the Kennedys, who had moved into a hotel so that Jackie and her family could stay there. On January 27, she moved her family to a house she had bought on the same street, number 3017.

Interview with Jamie Auchincloss contd
JACKIE'S HALF BROTHER
Ashland, Oregon, December 2004

In this section of his interview, Jamie Auchincloss recalls the night of Jack Kennedy's assasination.

On the afternoon of Jack's assassination, my mother had me flown down from school to Washington and taken to our Georgetown house to look after Jackie's children, Caroline and John. My mother had taken charge of them and taken them out of the White House to the safety of our home. I was seventeen years old, and knew John John and Caroline well as they often spent their vacations with us.

I was told why they were there, and that they had not been told yet that anything had happened. I was to play with them and had to suppress the biggest news of the century for about three hours. It was a pretty big burden, but they knew that I was one of the few people who could play with them. I couldn't let them see the television news.

There was a moment when Caroline left the room and ran into the maids' dining room where the Secret Service men were. They had the television on and a great number of weapons out on the table. I always knew the Secret Service carried guns, but usually you did not see them. That night we all saw them on display—pistols and big automatic weapons laid out. As Caroline ran in to get a cookie, they made a mad dash to the television set to turn it off and hide their weapons. She noticed that something was very different. That afternoon Caroline was meant to go off to her first sleep-over with someone from the White House nursery school. When she was in the car, the radio came on and the driver heard, 'shot in Dallas with his wife Jackie,' and quickly turned the radio off before Caroline realized.

Suddenly the Secret Service men in the car behind began making frantic signals, and she was driven back to the White House at high speed. She was only five years old. I felt so sorry for those little children. Caroline was smart; she knew something was very wrong.

That night my parents drove out to the naval hospital and spent seven or eight hours with Jackie as they did the autopsy on the president. They went back to the White House at four in the morning. Jackie asked my father to sleep in the president's bed, as she did not want it to be unoccupied. I remember thinking that was very spooky. But Jackie was so strong over those few days. She had the ability to give everyone else comfort and buck you up. Of course I did my best to show her I could be as strong as possible too.

When it really mattered, there was a very strong bond between my mother and Jackie. After the assassination, Jackie moved out of the White House to a house two blocks from ours, in Georgetown. She asked our mother to put two boxes in our attic: one dated September 12, 1953 and the other marked November 22, 1963.

Jackie had given my mother her wedding dress and her pink suit, the one Jack was assassinated next to, in those boxes. I think that act showed that Jackie knew that if that suit had gone into government storage, people would have found it and cut off the pieces of fabric with the president's blood on. When it came down to it, Jackie trusted my mother more than anyone else. She wouldn't have given those boxes to a person she didn't like or need.

chapter 4

Mourning Marriage Independence

Forging a future–1964 to 1975

Once Jackie had left the White House, Washington life was all but over for her. She initially had wanted to cling to the place where she and Jack had spent much of their married life—at one stage there was even a chance that Defense Secretary Robert McNamara could fix it for her to live in their pre-White House Georgetown home, but his plan did not come off. She had little desire to continue to engage in political life, though the symbolic power she possessed as the President's widow was enormous.

The new President, Lyndon Johnson, offered her the position of ambassador to France ten days after the assassination, which she immediately turned down. As Kennedy's press secretary Pierre Salinger said, "If she really wanted to keep some kind of a government link after she had been in the White House, if she really wanted to remain a public figure on her own, she would have accepted that job. But this is the end of it. Except for projects in memorial to the President."

In addition to working with architect John Carl Warnecke on the design of the President's grave at Arlington, which was engraved with lines from his speeches, Jackie's main priority was fundraising for the John F. Kennedy Presidential Library, which she set about with alacrity, pulling in large donations from wealthy acquaintances and foreign governments, and urging friends and staff to record oral histories. She appointed the architect I. M. Pei, whose previous work had been, by his own admission, mostly "unglamorous" slum-clearance projects. "It was really an emotional decision. He was so full of promise, like Jack; they were born in the same year."

She was also involved in establishing the Kennedy School of Government, later The Institute of Politics, at Harvard. But no project could distract Jackie from her grief, which was acute and violent—"I am a living wound," she described her condition to a friend. She would lash out in her suffering at those around her, her staff, and her sister, Lee. She felt vulnerable and exposed in 3017 N Street, where public and photographers would gather across the street hoping for a glimpse of her tragic figure.

Going away on trips with her children provided some slight relief; however it was "so empty and depressing to come home." In March 1964, she testified in front of the Warren Commission, poring over the events in Dallas once more—she hardly cared about the flurry of conspiracy theories or the supposed bias of the commission: "They could never bring back the person who was gone." With another version of the assassination set to be told in print by Jim Bishop, a reporter whom she disliked, Jackie appointed the historian William Manchester to write an authorized account of the assassination, granting him a highly personal interview.

She poured out her distressing personal recollections, all the while drinking daiquiris and chain-smoking, and later she forbade him to use the taped material (now embargoed until 2067). When Manchester completed the book, Jackie reacted to his account with hysterical fury, forcing months of revisions and negotiations, and eventually asking her lawyers to prevent the book's publication and serialization in *LOOK*. She eventually retreated, allowing the book to be published in April 1967, but by then, her legal battle against the writer whom she had authorized had somewhat compromised her image as the dignified and valiant widow.

Jackie announced, in July 1964, that she intended to move to New York and put the Georgetown house and their Virginia home, Wexford, up for sale. By September, with the help of financier André Meyer, Jackie had purchased a fourteen-room Coop.

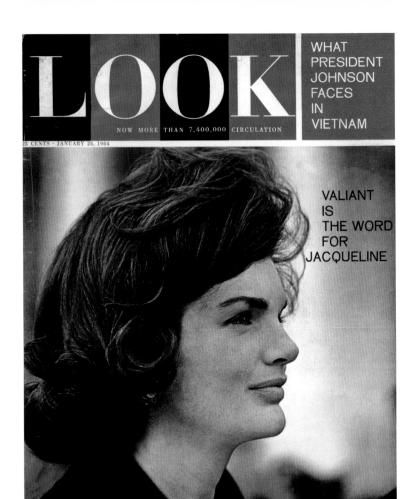

Above: **Jackie saluted on the cover of *LOOK* magazine—"Valiant is the word for Jacqueline." January 28, 1964**

The $200,000 apartment, at 1040 Fifth Avenue, was situated opposite Central Park. There, she and the children continued to receive Secret Service protection and she was surrounded by family—Lee, Peter and Pat Lawford, Stephen and Jean Smith, who also lived on Fifth Avenue; stepbrother Yusha on Park Avenue; and Bobby (who was running for the New York Senate) in the United Nations Plaza.

Jackie took Nancy Tuckerman and Pamela Turnure with her and stationed them in a government-financed, four-room office on Park Avenue. She also leased a weekend home in Peapack, New Jersey, where she could hunt. Washington became part of her past, and she continually refused Lyndon Johnson's invitations to return for various functions. Friends like John White, the Bradlees, and the Bartletts, who were part of the Kennedys' Washington circle, soon found that they no longer played a significant role in Jackie's life.

In 1965, Jackie began to emerge from her mourning, appearing in public more often with various escorts. She threw a lively party for J. K. Galbraith, the ex-ambassador to India, to thank him for his help on her trip two years previously, taking over a restaurant and decorating it with her own Indian-style paintings and lifesize cutouts of Galbraith. The guests included Andy Warhol and Edie Sedgwick. Jackie stayed until 2:45 A.M., dancing the frug and the watusi in a white crepe sheath dress and leaving with John Carl Warnecke.

Free from the political atmosphere of Washington, Jackie immersed herself in the artistic life of New York, making frequent trips to the theater and the ballet. She was friends for a spell with Truman Capote (although they later fell out), and she acquired many admirers in those circles—the poet Robert Lowell developed an obsessive love for her and Philip Roth accompanied her to small Manhattan dinner parties.

She became close to Alan Jay Lerner, who had written the lyrics to the musical *Camelot*, also to the set designer for the American Ballet Theater, Oliver Smith. Film director Mike Nichols was one of her more successful suitors. He commented to her once: "Taking you any place is like going out with a national monument." "Yes, but isn't it fun?" she replied. Jackie also had a relationship of mutual adulation with powerful financier André Meyer.

Throughout the late sixties, speculation constantly raged as to Jackie's romantic attachments, with the press often failing to keep up. Rumors of an engagement to the architect John Carl Warnecke were published after their relationship had petered out. Following the death of the wife of David Ormsby-Gore, the British ambassador to Washington, Jackie and David (by then Lord Harlech) shared a mutually consoling relationship. But though the press anticipated a union, their romantic involvement was fleeting, ending by the time he accompanied her to Cambodia in November. She had also gradually developed a serious relationship with the married deputy defense secretary, Roswell Gilpatric, who was by her side on a trip to the Yucatan peninsula to visit archaeological digs in March, 1968. While they were away, Bobby announced his plans to run for President.

Jackie already had another target—Aristotle Onassis, whom she had been seeing frequently. Gilpatric was aware of this: "She told me … she felt she could really count on Onassis, to be there for her and her children. That he was extremely protective of her … He could afford to build the buffers she then needed to ensure some degree of privacy." At the end of May, 1968, Onassis took Jackie on a cruise in the Virgin Islands. One week later, she returned when events took a shattering turn with the news that Bobby had been shot by a Palestinian gunman, Sirhan Sirhan, in Los Angeles, moments after winning the California primary on June 5.

Bobby had known and fiercely opposed Jackie's plans to marry Onassis, not merely because of his long-held animosity for Onassis, but also because of the political damage it would inflict upon him. "For God's sake, Jackie—this could cost me five states!" he fumed. But following Bobby's death, the Kennedys accepted that Jackie was going to go ahead—Ted Kennedy visited Skorpios with her that August to help devise a prenuptial agreement.

Only nineteen weeks after her brother-in-law's assassination in June, Jackie announced her intention to wed Aristotle Onassis (known as Ari). The ceremony took place on October 20, 1968 on Skorpios, with Ari's children, Christina and Alexander Onassis, and Caroline and John Kennedy among the close family looking on. Their marriage was widely perceived to be a transaction—with Jackie getting what she wanted in terms of serious money and privacy, and Ari acquiring the ultimate status accessory and a way back into America. Columnist Doris Lilly said: "He wanted to show the world … that he could buy anything or anybody."

Their relationship grew less happy as the years passed, and after Ari's son Alexander was killed when he crashed his hydroplane in January 1973, Onassis' despair and anger focused on Jackie. Divorce had been discussed and the Onassis family speculated that Jackie was a curse. "Christina … felt Jackie was somehow to blame," said Ari's friend Costa Gratsos. "Death was never very far from "the Black Widow" … Everybody around her had perished."

At this time, Onassis' health began to deteriorate, and he was diagnosed with myasthenia gravis, a muscle disorder. In early 1975, by which time Jackie and Ari were living almost entirely separate lives, he collapsed and was taken to hospital in Paris. Jackie commuted back and forth from New York to see him, but on March 17, when Aristotle Onassis died, his wife was a continent away.

I will tell you one thing. They will never drag me out like a little old widow, like they did Mrs. Wilson when President Wilson died. I will never be used that way ... I'm not going around accepting plaques. I don't want medals for Jack. I don't want to be seen by crowds.

Previous page: **Jackie, with Ted and Bobby Kennedy, making a televised statement from the Office of the Attorney General (Bobby Kennedy) January 14, 1964**

She thanked the public for the hundreds of thousands of letters of condolence, which she pledged to keep in the John F. Kennedy Presidential Library.

"The knowledge of the affection in which my husband was held by all of you has sustained me, and the warmth of these tributes is something that I will never forget," she said.

Left: **Jackie, John John, and Caroline laying a bouquet on Jack's grave at Arlington Cemetery, May 29, 1964**

The day would have been his forty-seventh birthday. Jackie was determined that Jack's birthday would be the date to be remembered, rather than the anniversary of his death. Later that day, she gave a televised address by satellite, making a plea for world peace.

Can anyone understand how it is to have lived in the White House and then, suddenly, to be living alone as the president's widow? There's something so final about it. And the children. The world is pouring terrible adoration at the feet of my children and I fear for them. How can I bring them up normally? We would never even have named John after his father if we had known ...

Right: **Jackie with John John on the porch of their Georgetown home, 3017 N Street, June 17, 1964**

Jackie's fourteen-room, Colonial-style home became a tourist attraction with gawkers lining the street at all hours of the day, some even setting up picnic tables across the road. There were also numerous photographers, whom Jackie likened to "locusts." Because the house was raised off the street, it was easy to see in through the windows, and she complained: "I can't even change my clothes in private because they can look into my bedroom window."

I remember going to the opera with her once ... the public curiosity about her was extraordinary. She said she wanted to go to the ladies' room. We walked out from behind the box and this enormous crowd followed her—into the ladies' room!

George Plimpton

Left: **Jackie with lyricist Alan Jay Lerner, New York December 7, 1964**
They are attending a performance of *On a Clear Day You Can See Forever* at the Mark Hellinger Theater. Lerner was one of the cultivated men who escorted Jackie after she moved to New York. It was Lerner's lyrics that had inspired Jackie to coin the Camelot legend of the White House. Lerner, who knew Jack Kennedy at school and Harvard, was skeptical about Jack's supposed love for his lyrics, because Jack had never mentioned the song to him.

I had forgotten, and my children have never known, what it is like to discover a new place, unwatched and unnoticed

Right: **Jackie, Caroline, and John John, with Lee and her son, Anthony Radziwill, outside Buckingham Palace, London, to watch the changing of the guard, May 1965**

Visiting London for the dedication of a memorial to Jack, Jackie made sure she took Caroline and John John to see the sights, including the Tower of London and London Zoo. While in London, the three had their portrait taken by Cecil Beaton.

Although the children did not know it, their stay in London was the last time they would spend with their British nanny, Maud Shaw, who had decided to retire because Caroline and John John were now both at school.

It was such an emotional and difficult day for me—so many thoughts of all my loss surged in me again

Left: **The Queen greets John John, Jackie, and Caroline at the dedication of the John F. Kennedy Memorial at Runnymede, England, May 14, 1965** David Ormsby-Gore (by then Lord Harlech), the former British ambassador to Washington and Kennedy friend, stands alongside Queen Elizabeth.

In the ceremony, the Queen gave an acre of British ground over to the USA, marked by a white stone monument, and both Jackie and Prime Minister Harold Macmillan delivered speeches.

To visit Seville and not ride horseback is equal to not coming at all

Right: **Jackie, with the Duchess of Alba, in traditional Andalusian dress (*traje corio*), riding a white stallion through Seville's spring fair, April 22, 1966**

On her visit to Seville, Jackie watched the "exciting and beautiful" fights in the city's bullring, where Spain's three leading bullfighters dedicated their animals to her. She was criticized by animal rights groups, but was unrepentant. Jay Rutherford, who reported on her trip, recalls: "Jackie was aware that donning the Andalusian riding habit would rile critics, but … she was anxious to avail herself of pleasure and privilege, and wasn't taking into account the consequences of public evaluation."

Next page: **Jackie at the private ceremony following the re-interment of the body of President Kennedy in the reconstructed grave site, Arlington National Cemetery, Virginia, March 16, 1967**

Above: **Caroline proudly names the USS *John F. Kennedy* at the Newport News Shipbuilding Yards, May 27, 1967**

The aircraft carrier cost $200,000,000 to build, and $300,000 was spent on the ceremony. Defense Secretary Robert McNamara gave the dedication address.

She was real with her kids
... She lived for her kids,
she would have done
anything for them

Peter Beard, photographer

> The visit is a very great contribution to a moral and sentimental rapprochement between—I do not say our two governments—but our two peoples.

Prince Sihanouk of Cambodia

Previous page: **Jackie, Caroline, and John John riding in Waterford, Ireland, June 16, 1967**

The family rented a large Georgian house, Woodstown, for a six-week "sentimental journey." Jackie said:"I'm so happy to be here, in this land my husband loved so much. For myself and the children, it is a little bit like coming home."

Right: **Jackie touring the ruins at Angkor Wat, Cambodia, with Lord Harlech in attendance, November 3, 1967**

Although most of the press were concentrating on the significance of Lord Harlech's presence in Cambodia, Jackie's semiofficial visit was designed for political ends. "Jackie was on a subtle, probing mission camouflaged as a tourist trip ... to pave the way for further diplomatic exchanges between Phnom Penh and Washington," reporter Marvin Kalb explained. Jackie, who was opposed to the escalation of the war in Vietnam, appealed to Prince Sihanouk of Cambodia to ask the Vietcong not to mistreat US prisoners of war. The prince made no firm commitment, but her visit went some way to reducing anti-American feeling.

Jackie, Bobby, lone motherhood

The intensity of Jackie's despair could only be understood by one person: Bobby. Publicly, between them, they were caretaking Jack's memory, making important decisions about how his legacy should be commemorated, and doing such things as designing his grave at Arlington. Privately, both were disabled by grief—Pierre Salinger described Bobby at that time as "the most shattered man I had ever seen in my life." Jackie and Bobby clung to one another.

Bobby took the role of surrogate father to Caroline and John John, spending time at Jackie's home and joining them on skiing trips and vacations. Bobby was able to put Caroline at her ease; because she was older, she had felt the blow of her father's death more fiercely and had become quiet and introverted. When reporters crowded around the car she was traveling in, she would hide on the floor saying, "Please tell me when nobody's looking." William Joyce, one of the other parents at the White House school, commented: "She was one of the wannest-looking children I've ever seen."

There were moments when Jackie felt her own misery would damage her children and considered sending them to live with Bobby and Ethel. A friend remembers that she quickly became set against such a notion. "She wants her children to realize that, even though the family is now reduced to three, it is still a unit and they still belong to the president and to her."

Roswell Gilpatric recalls how Bobby would try to lift Jackie out of her bleakest moods: "He'd get on the phone and say, 'Jackie get yourself feeling up! Don't just sit around there and mope!' He was very good in keeping up her morale and spirits when she might get into a depression." He also helped her financially, providing her with an extra $50,000 annual allowance.

Bobby had long admired his sister-in-law, saying of her years before: "She's poetic, whimsical, provocative, independent, and yet very feminine. Jackie has always kept her own identity and been different. That's important in a woman."

Jackie transferred the support she had given to Jack in his work directly to Bobby. When he faltered, wanting to drop out of politics in the months after Jack's death, Jackie sent him a heartfelt and persuasive letter urging him to persist. She helped him with his speech at the 1964 Democratic Convention. She would suggest interesting artists for him to meet, such as the poet Robert Lowell, and books for him to read.

On a trip to Antigua with a depressed Bobby, Lee's family, and Chuck Spalding, Jackie passed Bobby her copy of *The Greek Way* by Edith Hamilton—which had in fact been a gift sent to her by Aristotle Onassis. He disappeared to read it for hours on end, underlining passages and drawing particular comfort from Aeschylus' and Herodotus' insights into tragedy.

Jackie and Bobby made no attempt to conceal their numerous one-on-one meetings—reports read that they were "frequently spotted holding hands and whispering in darkened corners of … romantic clubs and restaurants"—as though the possibility of a romantic liaison between them was so unthinkable that they needn't worry about appearances. Within their circle, however, their relationship was certainly the subject of speculation.

Eunice Kennedy Shriver remarked to her sister-in-law, Ethel: "Well, what are you going to do about it? He's spending an awful lot of time with the widder." Mary DeGrace, who was on Ethel's staff at their Hyannis Port home, recalled: "There was more a feeling in the air than anything anyone actually saw. I would say it reached a peak during the summer of 1967, the year before Bobby got killed."

"Ethel felt threatened by Jackie. It seemed as though Bobby and Jackie were working up to something." Although, as Chuck Spalding observed, "Jackie and Bobby were as close as you can get," Jackie knew that in practical terms, her married brother-in-law could not be her future. Instead, she envisaged a life with Aristotle Onassis, who had been a sworn adversary of Bobby's since the early fifties, when Onassis believed that Bobby, then working on Senator Joe McCarthy's permanent sub-committee on investigations, had pursued a vendetta against him, raking up intelligence which resulted in a federal judgment that Onassis' ships would be seized when they docked at an American port. Some years later, as Attorney General, Bobby had banned Onassis from entering America.

In 1968 Bobby became a contender for the Presidency, and was concerned about the political fallout that such a marriage would incur. His contempt for Onassis ("He's a family weakness; first your sister and now you," he said to Jackie, having already warned Onassis off Lee when she was seeing him in 1963) was fulsomely returned. Referring to Jackie's relationship with Bobby, Onassis said to Yannis Georgiakis, his friend and chairman of Olympic Airways: "She doesn't know what she wants. Bobby's fucking up her mind the way he fucked up Monroe's."

When Jackie flew to Los Angeles and joined Ethel and the family at the Good Samaritan Hospital after hearing that Bobby had been shot, it was she who instigated turning off the life support machines that were keeping him alive but with no hope of recovery. "Nobody else had the nerve," recalled Bobby's aide, Richard Goodwin. Aristotle Onassis flew out to Los Angeles to comfort Jackie and accompanied her to New York, but was not invited to Bobby's funeral.

Above: **Jackie and Bobby featured on the cover of *Modern Screen* magazine, December, 1966**

I think I have a tendency to go into a downward spiral of depression or isolation when I'm sad. To go out, to take a walk, to take a swim, that's very much what the Kennedys do. It's a salvation, really.

Left: Jackie and John John skiing in Sun Valley, Idaho, on a trip with Bobby Kennedy, March 28, 1964

I suspect the one person she ever loved, if indeed she was capable of such an emotion, was Bobby Kennedy. Because Lee had gone to bed with Jack, symmetry required her to do so with Bobby. But there was always something oddly intense in her voice when she mentioned him to me.

Gore Vidal

Bobby was more to me than life itself

Left: **Jackie with Bobby Kennedy at the St. Patrick's Day Parade on Fifth Avenue, New York, March 17, 1966**

Jackie was standing on the street with Caroline and John John, but when Bobby came past in the parade she rushed to greet him, in a public show of her support. She said of him, "I'd jump out of the window for him."

Do you know what I think will happen to Bobby? The same thing that happened to Jack ... There is so much hatred in this country, and more people hate Bobby than hated Jack ... I've told Bobby this, but he isn't fatalistic like me.

Right: Jackie, sporting a campaign button, attends a rally for Bobby Kennedy with Roswell Gilpatric, deputy secretary of defense, the day before the California Primary, June 4, 1968

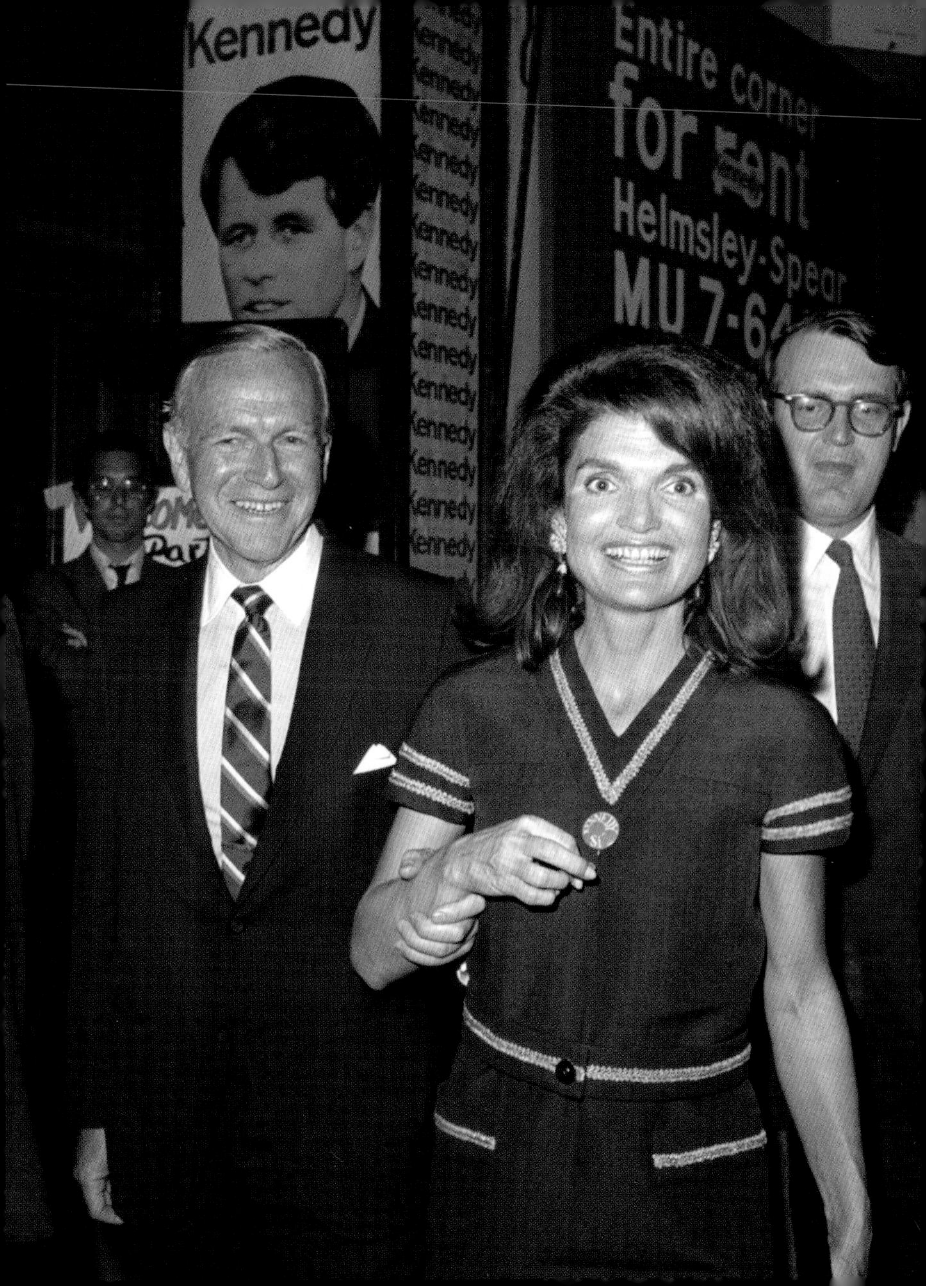
Kennedy
Entire corner
for
Helmsley-Spear

The Catholic Church understands death. I'll tell you who else understands death—the black churches. I remember at the funeral of Martin Luther King, I was looking at those faces, and I realized that they knew death ... We know death ... As a matter of fact, if it weren't for the children, we'd welcome it.

Left: **Jackie at the funeral service of Bobby Kennedy in St. Patrick's Cathedral, New York, June 8, 1968**

Jackie selected the music for the service with the help of her friend, Leonard Bernstein, and Ted Kennedy gave the eulogy. Standing next to her is Ralph Abernathy, best friend of Martin Luther King Jr. and fellow civil rights campaigner, and her sister, Lee. At Bobby's prompting, Jackie had attended the funeral of Martin Luther King Jr. in Atlanta when he was assassinated in April of that year.

His death was such a blow. I think she had a prop just taken from under her completely. She had to turn to somebody who could give her security. She so desperately needed security.

Roswell Gilpatric

Right: Jackie in prayer at the funeral service of Bobby Kennedy in St. Patrick's Cathedral, New York, June 8, 1968

The "Jackie O" look

Although following Jack's death, Jackie was more a focus of public attention than ever, she no longer felt the need to dress as a public figure. In her grief, just as she turned her back on Washington life, Jackie lost interest in the armorial and somewhat prim wardrobe she had managed so scrupulously while in the White House. When, one year after the assassination, she posed for *LOOK* photographer Stanley Tretick, she was utterly free of "the Jackie look" uniform— Jackie walked barefoot across the grass at Hyannis Port with her children, in a pair of loose slacks and yellow T-shirt. Her old friend from student days in Paris, Solange Herter, recalls her uncharacteristic lack of regard for her appearance when she saw her socially: "She wore the same old yellow dress—it was practically unraveling—for every single dinner party she gave at 1040 Fifth Avenue. I don't think she cared much about herself in those days."

But as Jackie's interest in clothes was rekindled, her tastes diversified. She had already started picking up the relaxed styles of the international jet set, sometimes via her sister Lee, before she was widowed. She had spent time with Rome-based designer Princess Irene Galitzine on Onassis' yacht in October 1963, and purchased her fluid silk palazzo pajama suits. She ditched her Kenneth Jay Lane three-strand faux pearl necklace for enamel pieces by Schlumberger.

On a trip to Rome in 1964, she first latched onto the designs of Valentino when, at a party, she spotted a Valentino ensemble worn by fellow guest Gloria Schiff. In September of that year, she ordered six dresses (in black and white as she was still in mourning), and started a friendship with the designer, who previously was little known outside Italy.

"At the beginning, I was Mr. Valentino and she was Mrs. Kennedy," he says. "Then it was Jackie and Valentino, and we became very, very close friends." He saw Jackie as being possessed of "a mix of naturalness and sophistication, an outdoorsy kind of beauty." Valentino made the fresh-looking two-piece of ivory georgette and lace that Jackie wore when she married Aristotle Onassis in 1968. He also dressed her for Onassis' funeral.

With her liberation from her dependence on the Kennedy clan for financial support, Jackie was able to further indulge her interest in fashion. She would shop compulsively, often directing bills to the Olympic Airways offices. Onassis gave her an allowance of $30,000 each month, which she would continually exceed—he eventually scaled it back to $20,000.

Truman Capote described her approach: "I accompanied her on one of those shop-till-you-drop sprees. She would walk into a store, order two dozen silk blouses in different shades, give them an address and walk out. She seemed in a daze, hypnotized." She became known in boutiques and department stores for often changing her mind about these lavish purchases—buying three dozen pairs of shoes on a trip to Bergdorf Goodman and returning them all the following day.

Alongside her untrammeled spending, Jackie sought to recoup some money by selling off her secondhand Yves Saint Laurent, Valentino, Halston, or Christian Dior, via the resale house Encore of New York, on Madison Avenue at 84th Street. This is a habit she had practiced since she was in the White House, when she used to use her secretary Mary Gallagher's name and address for the transactions. Jackie's tastes were unashamedly expensive. Onassis commented "She has an eye for immediately spotting the most precious and expensive object wherever she goes."

But yet, despite the head-turning baubles he would shower her with—the most ostentatious was perhaps the 40.42-carat diamond ring from Harry Winston—she would still gravitate toward more simple styles in her dress. Ari Onassis' close friend and business associate, Costas Gratsos, recalls: "He used to criticize her attire because all she wore were slacks and T-shirts. 'What the hell does she do with all the clothes she buys?' he used to ask."

Jackie would often go barefoot when in Greece, and elsewhere embraced basics such as white jeans worn with a black turtleneck. She used a Gucci bag—in canvas with leather-bound corners—which the design house later christened the Jackie bag.

She was engaged with the movement of fashion trends, wearing miniskirts and Yves Saint Laurent trouser suits, but as the late fashion commentator Eleanor Lambert said, "Jackie's taste was very unaffected, very distilled, and she had a sense of when to let go of a look."

The linchpins of her wardrobe were her sunglasses. She reputedly kept a basketful of pairs near the front door of her Fifth Avenue apartment to arm herself every time she left the house. Although she was vocal about protecting her privacy, her outsize, darker-than-dark lenses acted as an immediately recognizable signifier, rather than any kind of disguise, and the same went for her headscarves. Wearing them, she could attempt to shut out unwelcome attention, but she looked even more like the most famous woman in the world.

Right: **Jackie out shopping in Greece, 1971. She is wearing a bright yellow dress, trademark sunglasses, and carrying her Gucci "Jackie" bag**

Above: **Jackie in relaxed but elegant trenchcoat leaving Maxim's restaurant in Paris after lunch with Aristotle Onassis in 1974**

Left: **Jackie with Valentino, her favorite Italian fashion designer, strolling barefoot in Capri, August 1970**

Marriage to Onassis

Jackie's announcement on October 17, 1968, of her impending nuptials to Aristotle Socrates Onassis, was greeted with outrage in the press. "Jackie Weds Blank Cheque" read a British tabloid; "Jackie, How Could You?" read the *Stockholm Expressen*; "The Reaction Here is Anger, Shock and Dismay" exclaimed the *New York Times*.

The headlines mirrored the sentiments of her family. Yusha Auchincloss, Jackie's stepbrother, remarked, "I don't think we could ever understand, but we tried because we loved her." Rose Kennedy gave Jackie her support while professing to be "stunned" and "perplexed." Janet Auchincloss considered Onassis to be vulgar and disliked the way he had dropped Lee for Jackie, but her opposition to their match did not extend to boycotting the wedding or rejecting the diamond clip that Onassis bought for her from her jeweler, Zolotas.

By entering into marriage with Onassis, Jackie had willfully flung herself off the pedestal she had been standing upon throughout her public life. "It's better than freezing there," she said emphatically to Bunny Mellon. *Vogue* was one of the lone media voices to champion her, celebrating the explosion of the "lovely myths" surrounding the former First Lady and pronouncing: "The actual woman is far better—delectable, determined, emotional, strongly beautiful, questing."

Although Bobby had pledged to Jackie that she could wed Onassis once the presidential election was over, according to friends, he was still determined not to allow the marriage to go ahead at all. Onassis may have had to do more than thrash out an agreement with André Meyer to pay Jackie $3 million to secure her hand. In Peter Evans' revelatory book, *Nemesis* (2004), he tracks a series of machinations which connect Aristotle Onassis to the death of Bobby Kennedy. Three weeks before her death, Onassis' daughter, Christina, told Evans that Onassis had paid protection money for Olympic Airways to a Palestinian terrorist named Mahmoud Hamshari and had later found out that his money was used to assassinate Bobby in a high-profile gesture of revenge following the Six Days' War. Onassis had, in fact, met Hamshari on numerous occasions during 1968 and arranged to pay him a large sum, reportedly $1.2 million—several times the $300,000 Hamshari had originally demanded for the airline's protection.

Onassis' business associate, Costa Gratsos, summarized the resolution of Onassis' relationship with Bobby thus:

"Ari had always taken what he wanted, and for the first time in his life he had come up against a young man who was as tough, competitive, and determined as he was. And now that man was dead."

Once married, Jackie focused on enjoying the benefits of her new union. The couple spent their three-week honeymoon in near-total seclusion on Skorpios, punctuated by two trips to Athens (one for business) and a cruise on the *Christina* to Rhodes. Jackie brought Billy Baldwin to Skorpios to redecorate Onassis' home with lots of native wicker. She redesigned the gardens and then painted watercolors of them.

Ari's children, Christina and Alexander, neither of whom had a loving relationship with their business-obsessed father, strongly resented Jackie's invasion. Alexander pronounced: "Since my father married, I have no home." Onassis made considerable effort to make Caroline and John John feel at home, buying them gifts—John John, a speedboat, and Caroline, a white pony.

Jackie and Ari were physically passionate at the start of their marriage, and Onassis used to boast openly about their sex life. Despite this, he did not stop seeing his mistress, Maria Callas, with whom he had been involved since the late fifties when he was still married to his first wife, Tina. Callas had divorced her husband in 1959, in the hope of marrying Onassis herself, but he had never proposed. She found out about his marriage to Jackie when it was reported in the newspapers.

It was easy enough for Onassis to enjoy liaisons with Callas—Jackie seemed prepared to ignore the situation provided it did not embarrass her publicly. Jackie and Ari both lived nomadic existences; Jackie did not move full time to Skorpios—she knew Jack would have wanted her to raise Caroline and John John principally in the US. As for Ari, he was rarely on Skorpios for more than two days at a stretch. Onassis idealized their long-distance arrangement saying, "I have found that the longer the separation between us, the happier we are to meet again."

Jackie liked to invite her friends and family to Skorpios. Jackie loved Greece and had a romantic view of its "supernatural rapport with divinity." Janet and Hughdie came one summer, and Rose Kennedy visited three times during the first year of Jackie and Aristotle's marriage. Jackie's photographer friend Peter Beard recalls: "Great meals, fantastic picnics. It was lush—nonstop Dom Perignon and OJ."

Right: **Jackie with her second husband Aristotle Onassis dining out in New York, October 7, 1970**

She expressed her entrancement with her life change to her friend Vivian Crespi: "Do you realize how lucky we are, Vivi? To have gotten out of that world we came from. That narrow world of Newport. All that horrible anti-Semitism and bigotry. Going every day to that club with the same kinds of people. You and I have taken such a big bite out of life."

But as the months wore on, it was clear that the bond between Jackie and Ari was becoming increasingly tenuous. Not only were they rarely in the same city, let alone the same bed, but Onassis was exasperated by her spending habits and resentful that she would expect him to pay for huge amounts of clothes, trinkets, and lawyer's bills over and above his $30,000 monthly allowance. By the end of 1972, the pair were hardly communicating.

After January 22, 1973, the day twenty-four-year-old Alexander Onassis was killed while training his father's personal pilot in a hydroplane, Ari was never the same again. "Alexander's death destroyed him. He was convinced his enemies had plotted the act," recalls Costa Gratsos. Onassis could not share his grief with Jackie—with his superstitions about a Kennedy curse, part of him blamed her. All there was between them was anger and unhappiness. "I saw the biggest fights between them you could ever imagine. He would blow up all the time—tantrums about everything. Yelling and screaming at her," said Peter Beard.

Spending yet more time apart from Onassis and preoccupied with events to mark the tenth anniversary of the Dallas assassination Jackie did not notice the signs of serious illness—his tiredness, his weight-loss, his drooping left eyelid, which he eventually resorted to keeping open with a Band-Aid. He was suffering from myasthenia gravis, a serious disease affecting his muscles. Jackie did not show much concern—as his health deteriorated, the relationship continued to do so also. Onassis drafted a will that would give Jackie an income of $200,000 per year for life.

Onassis began making detailed preparations to spring a divorce action on Jackie. In February 1975, he collapsed in Athens with chest pains, and Jackie contacted a cardiologist who insisted Onassis be transferred to a Paris hospital, where his gall bladder was removed. Jackie went to Paris to be near him while he was kept on a respirator, but in the first week of March, asked a doctor whether Onassis was stable enough for her to leave for a few days. Despite his opinion that she should stay in Paris, Jackie flew back to New York. Aristotle Onassis died of bronchial pneumonia on March 15 with Christina beside him.

After his funeral on March 18, The *New York Times* reported that Onassis had intended to divorce Jackie before he died. Jackie demanded that Christina make a statement denying this, which she duly did despite the fact that it was true. That was not all that Jackie wanted from Christina, however. She entered into a dispute with Christina over Onassis' $1 billion estate, attempting to claim a larger share. Christina offered her a settlement for over $20 million, which she accepted. Jackie had the money to buy as much freedom and security as she would ever need.

Next page: **Jackie strolling barefoot alongside Aristotle Onassis' yacht, the *Christina*, with her family, October 19, 1968**
This was the day before she married Onassis on his 350-acre private island off the west coast of Greece, Skorpios.

I can't very well marry a dentist from
New Jersey

Had she married just anybody,
she'd probably have remained
exposed to the curiosity of the world.
She loved Onassis. Onassis was rich enough
to offer her a good life and powerful enough
to protect her privacy.

Lee

Left: **Aristotle and Jackie Onassis, with her ten-year-old daughter
Caroline, following the Greek Orthodox wedding ceremony in the tiny
Chapel of the Little Virgin, October 20, 1968**
Jackie's stepfather, Hughdie, gave her away at the evening ceremony,
where Onassis' children Christina and Alexander stood close to one
another with "unhappy, angry faces." The wedding party emerged into the
cold, rainy evening and were showered with rice and sugared almonds.
They went on to hold a reception on board the *Christina*.

Above: **Jackie and Ari sailing off Skorpios in the weeks following their marriage, October, 1968**

Right: **Jackie swims in the Ionian sea off Skorpios alongside Aristotle Onassis' yacht, ten days after her wedding, October 30, 1968**

A few days after the wedding, he was back in Paris whistling under Maria's window.

Robert Sutherland, friend of Maria Callas

Above: **Jackie and Maria Callas on the cover of** *Photoplay*, **July 1970**

Right: **A contented Jackie and Ari relaxing in Greece,** *circa* **1970**
Ari is reading a lexicon of Greek dialects.

She was like a hungry vulture waiting to feast on my father's flesh. I wanted to get as far away from her as possible.

Christina

Left: **Jackie and Christina Onassis arrive at Aktion airport from Paris with Onassis' body, March 18, 1975**

Next page: **Jackie holds hands with John John and Caroline by Onassis' coffin at his funeral in the Chapel of the Little Virgin on Skorpios, March 18, 1975**

While traveling in the automobile to Nidri before the funeral, Teddy Kennedy, who was escorting Jackie, confronted Christina saying: "Now, what about the money?"

Interview with Ron Galella
PAPARAZZI PHOTOGRAPHER
London, December 2004

Galella is a photographer whose trademark is his "off-guard" pictures of celebrities. Jackie was his most prized subject of all, and his relentless pursuit of her from New York to Skorpios ended in a courtroom in 1972, with a highly publicized battle. Andy Warhol described Ron Galella as his favorite photographer for "being in the right place at the wrong time."

My first take of Jackie was in May 1967, at the Wildenstein Gallery in New York, at an Italian art opening. She was there with André Meyer, her financier friend. It was very crowded inside, but when she left, another photographer knew where her apartment was and so we beat her to the apartment in my car and got better pictures, with nobody in the way. So that's when I learned where she lived. I could hang out there.

I only photographed her twice in 1967, that evening and then on December 10, 1967, at a big Democratic Party benefit $500 plate dinner at the Plaza Hotel. She was there with Averell Harriman, Cary Grant, Robert Kennedy, and Ted Kennedy.

After two or three months, she recognized me. That was the only time she touched me. At the beginning of 1968, I went to the 21 Club; she was there with Ari Onassis. Jackie came out and I was there, taking a picture. She grabbed my wrist and pushed my elbow into the limousine and she whispered, "You've been hunting me for three months now." I said, "Yeah, yeah … of course." I was shocked that she said it. After that her remark was usually: "Oh, it's you again." I would hang out near her apartment to see if she would go out in the evening—her favorite restaurants were La Côte Basque and the 21 Club. I dated her maid, Greta Neilsen, for a while, and she would tell me things like when Jackie was going to go and get her hair done.

I once took a whole series of pictures of her in a Chinese restaurant in Chinatown when she was there with I. M. Pei, the architect of the Kennedy Library, Doris Duke, and Ari. The maître d' invited me in to take pictures so I sat near the coat rack in the restaurant and then I took pictures from behind the coat rack, just using the available light.

She played tricks with me too. Once I went to the 21 Club and got out of the car ahead of her. Her car made to pull up and then pulled away quickly. She enjoyed beating me, losing me. I would sometimes go to Peapack, New Jersey, where she spent weekends. I took pictures of her with Caroline and John John at a horse show.

I spent at least a month near Skorpios in 1970, at a little town on the mainland, Nidri. There were only two hotels and I picked the better one. Jackie's Secret Service agents were staying there too. When I wasn't in my room, my traveler's checks went missing—a dirty trick—so I had to go all the way back to Athens to the American Express office to get my money back. I smuggled myself onto the island on a Greek fishing boat, dressed as a sailor—I hid in the hold with fumes and carbon monoxide coming in on me from the exhaust. I got some pictures of her swimming in the sea. While I was there I went over to Capri for two days and followed her and Lee.

Next page: **Galella taking the last of a long sequence of Jackie photographs in New York, October 7 1971**

They were on a shopping trip. She bought magazines including one with a picture of Ari and Maria Callas kissing on the cover. When they were sitting in a café, she ordered a waiter to call the police to get rid of me. I left her a bit, as it is never good to stay around when somebody gets mad at you. Later I saw Ari and he spoke to me, surprised that I traveled all over. He could be friendly, he loved publicity—very different from Jackie.

Jackie was my ideal subject because she was always doing something. She would go out with men; she would go walking, jogging, shopping. And she was ignoring me which is good. I never felt guilty that I was overdoing it because she would just carry on. Most celebrities would say, "Come on, take my picture" and then you have to say, "Goodbye, thank you"; it's over. "Pose, smile—that's it." Jackie didn't do that. I loved that.

Elizabeth Taylor was my other main subject at the time—I have more photographs of her than of Jackie (4,000 of her; 3,000 of Jackie). Elizabeth Taylor was much easier. She was much nicer, much more obliging and easy to stop and [get her to] pose for you.

The year 1971 was my best year shooting Jackie—I took her twenty times. I made $40,000 altogether that year—$20,000 from Jackie, $20,000 from other celebrities.

The legal trouble started when I took that picture of her and John John on the bike from the bushes in Central Park in September, 1960. She claimed I jumped out at John John and made him swerve. Her Secret Service agent Connolly was also on a bike and he stopped me, saying, "You've had enough," and I stopped. Then Jackie said to him: "Smash his camera!" The other agents, Kalafatis and Walsh, ran after me and arrested me. They said if I gave them the film then they wouldn't arrest me. But I didn't give them the film, and they arrested me. I thought it was a false arrest.

She wanted her privacy and more than anything privacy of the children. Most of the time she was never really angry when I was taking the pictures of her, but because it was John Jr. I photographed, she didn't want those pictures to be released.

I stuck out my neck. I filed a $1.3 million dollar lawsuit for the interference with my work—for the false arrest by the Secret Service and their obstructing me. I sued her thinking she would settle out of court for a few thousand dollars. I didn't think she would go to court, because it would mean more publicity. But she went to court. She was strong-willed and she thought that she should get me, because other paparazzi did worse in Europe: they got her nude in Skorpios. I believe she did it to set an example, to prove a point—she was angry not just at me.

She did not accept herself as a celebrity. She thought that because she wants to be private, she is private, even when walking in public areas. I never went in her house, never shot through her windows—that's private. She moved to NY because in Washington after the assassination she lived in Georgetown; she had paparazzi on her doorstep every day. In New York there were no paparazzi every day, except when I came. She didn't like that.

She didn't believe that she was an actress, although she was. Even her getting into a limousine was like watching a one-act play. She was very aware, very mysterious. She was clever that way. That's why she would talk softly—you want to hear more when someone talks softly, it's more interesting than being loud. She knew all these tricks. And she used them in court too.

The court battle lasted twenty-six days in 1972, and she was there at least twenty days. The press thought it was very trivial that all this ended up in court. Jackie had a very distinguished team of lawyers—two floors' worth in Park Avenue in New York.

I could never win. It cost her $500,000 dollars, which she tried to get Ari to pay—he got them down to $235,000. The judge placed an injunction on me—I couldn't go within 100 yards of her apartment, I had to stay 50 yards from her to take a picture; 75 yards from the children. I appealed against the decision and in 1973 it was reduced. I was free to walk in front of her house and the 50 yards was reduced to 25 feet, and the distance from the children to 30 feet.

Later, in 1982, I broke the restriction when Jackie was going to the Winter Garden theater with Maurice Tempelsman to watch Twyla Tharp and was brought up before the same judge. I surrendered all rights to photograph Jackie or the children and was fined $10,000. I felt like I was missing out not being able to photograph her after that.

In a way I'm thankful because she picked me. I didn't think she was going to go to trial but she did and that made me infamous. Jackie was an opportunist and I am too—we have something in common. I'm an opportunist to get pictures and she was an opportunist to get money by marrying Onassis, by dating the men she dated—André Meyer helped her get the coop apartment at 1040 Fifth Avenue.

I was in awe of her. She was a former First Lady. I was a gentleman toward her; I don't believe I was ever nasty. I respected her highly. There was a love, but not a sexual kind of love. It was a love of photography, a subject that is interesting. Pursuing that is an adventure. I loved that. She was my most favorite subject.

Left: **Jackie asks a waiter to have Galella arrested, as he photographs her in an outdoor cafe, in Capri, August 24, 1970**

Publicity is like rain. When you're soaking wet, what difference do a few drops more make?

Aristotle Onassis, to Jackie

Right: Jackie making the cover of *LIFE* again, this time for her "Silly Courtroom Battle" with paparazzo photographer Ron Galella, March 31, 1972

LIFE

Silly courtroom battle

JACKIE vs. THE JACKIE WATCHER

Mrs. Onassis arrives at court

MARCH 31 · 1972 · 50¢

chapter 5

Freedom
Fun
Fulfillment

Peace at last—1975 to 1994

After Onassis' death in 1975, Jackie returned to Manhattan, the most famous widow in the world once again. Though extremely wealthy, her "primeval fear of poverty" at last laid to rest, Jackie could not for long be satisfied by lunches, trips to her psychoanalyst, visits from her acupuncturist, and watching people in Central Park through the telescope she had set up by the window of her apartment at 1040 Fifth Avenue.

Jackie had already started making an invaluable contribution to preserving New York's historic buildings—a cause which had concerned her since she had been a pivotal figure in the saving of Lafayette Square in Washington D.C. when she was First Lady. When she heard of Penn Central Railroad's plans to demolish Grand Central Station and sell the site for an office tower, Jackie joined the board of the Municipal Arts Society to oppose it fiercely. She used her public profile effectively—showing up at press conferences, rallies, and benefits. A lighting ceremony, highlighting the station's facade, was held on the same night as the opening of the Democratic Convention. Jackie turned on the switch and stole all the next day's front pages.

"Here was the Municipal Arts Society … with members that tended to be society types. It hadn't been a populist organization," remarked Kent Barwick, president of the MAS. "Jackie changed all that. People were touched by the idea of saving this building."

Jackie's personal and passionate response to such issues held real sway—whether it was campaigning to save the 1952 blue glass Lever House on Park Avenue, or arguing over the planned height of skyscrapers that would cast mile-long shadows across Central Park: "They're stealing our sky," she said.

In September 1975, Jackie made a vital life change. For the first time since she handed in her notice to Frank Waldrop at the *Washington Times-Herald* in 1953, she went out to work. Thomas Guinzberg, a friend whom she had first met while in Paris in the early fifties, was president of the publishing house Viking, and offered her a position as a consulting editor. She was to work in the publishing industry, first for Viking and then for Doubleday.

Jackie's social life consisted largely of attending various cultural events—she was a supporter of the Costume Institute at the Metropolitan Museum of Art and of the American Ballet Theater—and holding small dinner parties at her apartment. Her celebrity did not diminish with the years, and despite her own efforts, people found it almost impossible not to be phased by her fame. Former *LIFE* correspondent Richard Meryman described the "Jackie effect" on a dinner party at his home: "Nobody really talked to her. She seemed to have this strange hold on some very sensible, normal, articulate people … It's a presence that she brings into a room, an extraordinary aura of all the historic events connected to her."

Andy Warhol described the experience of visiting a Brooklyn Museum exhibition of Egyptian antiquities with her. "You could hear her name in the air: 'Jackie … Jackie … Jackie.' Somehow she managed to concentrate on the exhibition … to mentally block out all those intrusive onlookers." However, Warhol also remembers Jackie's penchant for gossip about other celebrities: "I'd recently appeared in a movie, *The Driver's Seat*, starring Elizabeth Taylor. "What's Elizabeth Taylor really like?" Jackie kept asking …"

Jackie's lifelong friend and right-hand woman, Nancy Tuckerman, recalls a fascination with Greta Garbo. "She was always excited to see Garbo, and to update me. "I saw her today again! Just walking along by herself," Jackie would say. "She's so mysterious!"

Jackie had no desire to fuel her own status as a public figure, and she resisted political offers such as the role of New York cultural affairs commissioner. She would only show her face out of loyalty to the Kennedys—she attended the Democratic Convention in 1976 when Sargent Shriver announced his candidacy (she also donated $25,000 to his campaign), and four years later campaigned with Teddy Kennedy—both men were unsuccessful in winning the presidential nomination. Beyond that kinship, Jackie was unwilling to be utilized politically. After President Jimmy Carter stepped up and kissed her at the opening of the John F. Kennedy Library in 1979, she commented archly to Arthur Schlesinger: "Isn't that strange the way we hardly knew each other, and the president kissed me? I suppose he thought he had *droit de seigneur.*"

Jackie was criticized by some for largely restricting her charitable energies to the arts and historical preservation—the only ongoing community initiative she actively promoted was the Bedford-Stuyvesant project in Brooklyn, which had been begun by Bobby Kennedy.

Sartorially, she maintained an elegant regal image as the years advanced, still discovering new designers—her favorite couturier Valentino was succeeded by Carolina Herrera in the early eighties, and she later switched hairdressers from Kenneth, whom she had known since the 1950s, to Thomas Morrissey, a former Kenneth employee who had set up his own salon. She reportedly had an eyelift when she entered her fifties (which went entirely unnoticed by the press), and a facelift when she reached sixty.

Her life had reached a happily settled keel, with her children growing up and away at college and a blossoming, yet determinedly low-key relationship with Maurice Tempelsman, an influential figure who had made his wealth as a diamond industry pioneer.

Jackie continued to spend time at Hyannis Port, visiting her mother-in-law, Rose Kennedy, and going hunting in New Jersey as well as later reestablishing her links with hunts near Middleburg, Virginia—where she would go and stay alone in a cottage near Bunny Mellon's house and "subsist on Lean Cuisine and candy bars." In 1981, she found her ultimate refuge from the exposure of city life when she bought several hundred acres near Gay Head on the southern tip of Martha's Vineyard.

"Jackie loved it when she first saw its oceanfront dunes, ponds, farmland, and, of course, the ocean itself. It was big enough to be completely private and the Vineyard didn't have a history for her," said her friend Rose Styron. Jackie commissioned architect Hugh Newell Jacobsen to create a home formed of connected pavilions, and named it Red Gate Farm. Each year, she would spend the summer there, sailing on Maurice Tempelsman's yacht, the *Relemar*, kayaking, birdwatching, or seeing the friends she made locally, such as Carly Simon—to whom she was like a big sister.

In these years of personal stability, Jackie offered support to those around her who were rocked by their circumstances—she acted as a confidante for Joan Kennedy, who was struggling with her husband Teddy's extramarital affairs and her own alcoholism. When her half-sister, little Janet, fell ill with cancer at thirty-nine, Jackie went to her bedside and was with her when she died at the Beth Israel Hospital in Boston. She was a patient and reliable source of care for her mother Janet, who suffered from Alzheimer's for years before she died in June, 1989. "Jackie was beyond extraordinary the last seven years of our mother's life," Lee said. "She really focused on her. It was very difficult to deal with her. I don't know too many children who would have behaved better and been more certain of her comfort, attention, and care."

Jackie had shown few signs of slowing—jogging around the reservoir in Central Park and riding to hounds (she fell off her horse and was knocked unconscious in November 1993)—when she herself became ill in late 1993. On a post-Christmas Carribean cruise with Maurice Tempelsman, she felt acute pains in her stomach and groin and flew back to New York for tests, where she was diagnosed with non-Hodgkin's lymphoma. Nancy Tuckerman made a press announcement on February 11, 1994.

To her friends and colleagues, she remained upbeat and hopeful about her prospects. She laughingly said to Arthur Schlesinger, "I feel it is a kind of hubris. I have always been proud of keeping so fit … and now suddenly this happens."

Her pursuit of her normal life was so convincing to those around her that it belied the severity of her condition. She carried on working at Doubleday. "Sometimes, she had Band-Aids on, and bruises from the therapy, but she carried on with her projects until the end," remembers her editorial assistant Scott Moyers. She continued campaigning against the construction of a Disney theme park near Middleburg ("I pray against Disney every night"), she played with her grandchildren in Central Park, she kept lunch dates. Her friend Edna O'Brien said: "She was secretive about her life and she was secretive about her death."

She was taken to hospital on Monday May 16, where it was discovered that the cancer had spread to her liver. Jackie discharged herself on Wednesday, and on Thursday evening at her apartment, with Maurice Tempelsman and her children near, she went to sleep and died.

Right: **Jackie attends a tribute to Josephine Baker at the Metropolitan Opera House, November 7, 1976**

Is it not cruel to let our city die by degrees, stripped of all our proud monuments, until there will be nothing left of all her history and beauty to inspire our children?

Jackie, writing to Mayor Abraham Beame

Left: **Jackie outside Grand Central Station January, 1975**
She is with (from left) architect Philip Johnson, TV personality Bess
Myerson, and Congressman Ed Koch, launching the campaign to save
Grand Central Station. Jackie attended this press conference a week before
Aristotle Onassis collapsed and was rushed to hospital.

I think my biggest achievement is that, after going through a rather difficult time, I consider myself comparatively sane

Right: **Jackie riding with the Essex Hunt Club in New Jersey on Thanksgiving, November 25, 1976**

She rode at Thanksgiving every year until 1993—that year she had fallen from her horse at a hunt earlier in November and been knocked out.

She was an actress and she liked to act. Almost everything she did had a premeditated quality about it. A sort of dramatic, theatrical quality which she enjoyed enormously.

Jay Mellon

Left: **Jackie attending the gala opening for the Costume Institute show at the Metropolitan Museum of Art, "Costumes of the Hapsburgs," accompanied by Hugh Fraser, December 3, 1979**
Hugh Fraser had been a beau of Jackie's in London from when she had first visited Europe. In 1975, he hosted Caroline at his house in Notting Hill while she did an art course at Sotheby's.

> She was loyal and supportive, but also concerned for my welfare … she told me to make time in the campaign for my family and to set aside time to get much-needed rest, and she was right

Teddy Kennedy

Right: **Jackie campaigning with Teddy Kennedy at the market in Spanish Harlem, New York, on the eve of the New York State Primary. March 24, 1980**

Jackie proved a hit when she spoke in Spanish to the people in Spanish Harlem, just as she had done when campaigning for Jack twenty years earlier. She also attended a Greek-American fundraiser in Queens and upon hearing their bouzouki music joked, "I'm homesick!"

The Teddy Kennedy campaign was overshadowed by his involvement in, and subsequent cover-up of, an incident when a girl drowned in his car at Chappaquiddick eleven years before. Jackie was convinced he would not win in New York and called a meeting of Kennedy associates at her apartment to see if they could persuade him to drop out. She did not get involved in the campaign until its last day. Teddy did win New York after Jackie's appearances, but more because opinion had swung against Jimmy Carter than because it had swung toward Teddy.

Her life in the last fifteen years seemed to me to be the most satisfying. It seems that her happiness in that period of time quadrupled.

Lisa Drew, editor

Left: **Jackie with Caroline at the American Ballet Theater gala at the Lincoln Center, New York, May 4, 1980**

New role

It was Letitia Baldridge, Jackie's social secretary in the White House, who suggested that she find herself a job in publishing. "I told Jackie, "You need a job." She had such a brilliant mind which needed to be challenged. It certainly was in the White House years. After that—nothing. She could have taught classes, but she didn't want to have to show up at a certain time. She became very anti-scheduling," Baldridge said.

The president of the publishing company Viking, Thomas Guinzberg, a friend of Jackie's since the 1950s through Lee's then husband Mike Canfield, knew that she (and her contacts) would be "a boon" to his company despite her lack of experience in the field, and he also understood that he would have to allow her to create her own routine.

Few at Viking expected her to be much more than a token addition to the staff when she started on September 22, 1975, at a salary of $10,000, amid the inevitable media storm and Viking staff "suddenly … reporting to work in their Guccis and pearls." However, Barbara Burn, an editor who worked with Jackie, said:

"After she arrived, we were all pleasantly surprised that she wasn't a stuffed shirt with a funny voice. She was really very serious about what she did … She was willing to roll her sleeves up and learn."

Jackie applied herself to work on a wide range of titles; some of the most high-profile ones were linked to exhibitions at the Metropolitan Museum of Art. She took the opportunity to travel widely to fully engage with the books' subject matter, visiting Russia, India, and China—"Being an editor," she said, "expands your knowledge and heightens your discrimination. Each book takes you down a different path." The level of her personal interest was reflected in her hands-on approach with some of her writers. Gita Mehta, whose brother Naveen Patnaik wrote *A Second Paradise: Indian Courtly Life 1590–1947* for Jackie, observed:

"[She was] really an extraordinary, nineteenth-century type of editor … Jackie sent Naveen pages of research and material annotated by herself. It was obscure research. I know as a writer that to have that kind of attention by a commissioning editor is quite rare."

Jackie's relationship with Viking ended on a somewhat sour note when the company published a novel by Jeffrey Archer, *Shall We Tell the President*. It told the tasteless tale of an assassination attempt on Teddy Kennedy, imagined by Archer as a second Kennedy president. Guinzberg claimed to have warned Jackie about the book, but when it was published (to condemnation) and Jackie was the subject of a barbed comment in the *New York Times*, she denied all knowledge to the press. She resigned and several months later, in February 1978, began working for Doubleday.

The range of titles she worked on at Doubleday was sweeping. As well as artistic and historical books reflecting her own interests, part of her remit was to secure celebrity autobiographies—one of her biggest coups was signing Michael Jackson, a process so frustrating and complicated (he stood her up for their first meeting at a Hollywood restaurant) that she complained it would give her an ulcer. J. C. Suarès, the designer of the resulting book, *Moonwalk*, recalled: "She kept asking me if he was gay. She was really fascinated by his sexual orientation. She never quite figured it out."

Sometimes these collaborations were a labor of love. Over time, she coaxed ballerina Gelsey Kirkland—then addicted to cocaine—to write her moving, bestselling autobiography, *Dancing on My Grave.*

"She helped me recover my life and my career. This was no small gift," Kirkland said. "She was both an editor and a friend, and whenever the two roles came into conflict, the friendship and affection won out."

Working in the office with Jackie, her assistant had to filter her mail (which could contain anything from a gun to marriage proposals for her son), as well as her calls. She had a separate line to which unidentified callers would be directed, known as the "kook line."

Her colleagues recall that, in her work, she was no more remote than she needed to be. Fellow Doubleday editor, Bruce Tracy, said:

"It was never beneath Jacqueline Onassis to always make her own phone calls. She always greeted her own guests. As often as not, she wrote her letters by hand. She avoided putting distance between herself and those she had business with."

As Stephen Rubin, the president of Doubleday, recalled, the only thing that would precipitate a retreat would be treating her like a celebrity. "An invisible shield would slam down and you wouldn't get through. She would close down in a way that was absolutely chilling and terrifying."

Particularly happy consequences of her work were the friendships she developed in later life. Jackie's work gave her an excuse to seek out people who fascinated her, such as *Rolling Stone* editor Joe Armstrong, or writer Edna O'Brien, just as she had done when inviting artists to the White House. This time the bonds she forged were close and transforming. Jane Hitchcock, who led a Bible reading at Jackie's funeral, said: "She became a surrogate mother to me and certainly taught me how to behave. She was the standard by which I measured myself."

Above: **Jackie in the Studio Books division of Viking Press, January 17, 1977**

She is with (from left) Christopher Holme, Gael Towey Dillon, and Bryan Holme. Bryan Holme, creative designer of the Studio Books division, which produced coffee table books, worked with Jackie on her first major project, *In the Russian Style*. He helped her negotiate the steep learning curve when she started in publishing.

He remembers, "She used to come into our office and watch us put together our books. She asked loads of questions. I'd answer them and her eyes would light up, 'I didn't know that. That's fascinating,' she would say. That's how she learned about publishing."

The book capturing the lavish culture of Imperial Russia was the accompaniment to an exhibition at the Costume Institute of the Metropolitan Museum of Art, curated by Diana Vreeland.

Keep your secret. That's your power over others

Diana Vreeland

Left: **Jackie being embraced by Diana Vreeland at the launch of Vreeland's book, *Allure*, New York, 1980**

Jackie worked on this book of arresting images of women accompanied by Vreeland's vivid commentary. It included shots of Marilyn Monroe and Maria Callas—of one photograph of Callas, Vreeland said, "If eyes were bullets, everyone in sight would be dead."

Since Diana Vreeland had been ousted as editor of *Vogue* in 1971, Jackie had looked out for her interests. In 1972, Jackie was one of a small group of contributors who funded a special salary for Vreeland so that the Metropolitan Museum could afford to appoint her as special consultant to the Costume Institute. In an essay by Jackie about Vreeland's work there, she described her as "whippet-boned with black, lacquered hair; looks like a high priestess, which in a way she is; and her temple is on the ground floor of the Metropolitan Museum of Art."

Right: **Jackie, emerging from a showing of *Death in Venice* at the Hollywood Twin Theater on 8th Avenue, July 21, 1981**

On the same day, Ron Galella had caught Jackie leaving the cinema. She later cited the incident when she testified against Galella in court in 1982, claiming he broke the restrictions about keeping at a certain distance.

"He was at least as close as a foot. I tried to hail a taxi … He was jumping all around me, in front and in back, and very close at times, so no taxi could see me. Every time I raised my arm, he'd be in front of me."

Jackie loved watching films and had catholic tastes, from the works of Fassbinder to *Tootsie*, which she was so desperate to see when it was released that she and Vivian Crespi sat in the aisle to watch it when they turned up at a sold-out showing.

Next page: **Jackie with feminist campaigner and editor of *Ms. Magazine*, Gloria Steinem, New York, May 16, 1984**

In 1979, she was interviewed by Gloria Steinem and appeared on the cover of *Ms. Magazine*. She had supported the magazine through private donations for some time, but had never stood up as a public supporter of Women's Liberation.

Gloria Steinem said of her approach:

"Jackie practiced feminism by being herself and helping other women be themselves. She became secure enough to do so. To like other women, you have to first like yourself and not feel competitive. She continued to mean something to women in general because she didn't continue to play the role of widow, politically or socially. When she went to work, she essentially did what she would have done if she had never been married and was on her own."

Proud mother and grandmother

In the mid-seventies, various revelations about Jack began to emerge—his affairs with Marilyn Monroe, Judith Campbell, and Mary Meyer, and his (and Jackie's) use of Dr. Max Jacobson's (aka Dr Feelgood) amphetamine-laced injections during the White House years. Jackie made strenuous efforts to reinforce a positive memory of Jack in their children. In their apartment, she pinned a world map on the wall to show Caroline and John all the places that she and Jack had visited during his presidency, and she asked Pierre Salinger, Kennedy's press secretary, to tell them stories about Jack's work. Caroline covered one wall in her room with pictures of her father and kept stamps that bore his image.

Caroline and John led advantaged yet disciplined lives. Their Secret Service agents were a constant presence, escorting them to school each day (Caroline to Brearley, John to Collegiate) to ensure their safety from kidnapping threats. Caroline had a similar reserve and quick intelligence to her mother, whereas the charismatic John was gregarious, making friends in minutes.

As Jackie had previously resisted her children being absorbed into the amorphous Kennedy clan after Jack died, so she continued to keep them distinctly separate from Ethel and the late Bobby's children, who had grown up "abandoned and treated with money and privileges." While they were young, the brood had dubbed themselves the Hyannis Port Terrors. The atmosphere was hedonistic and less than disciplined; David went on to die of a heroin overdose in April 1984.

However much she wanted them to avoid such curses of wealth, Jackie did not shelter Caroline and John from adventure. In fact, she was keen to toughen up John, whom she felt was a little too easygoing for his own good, and she asked a Secret Service agent to give him boxing lessons. When John was once mugged in Central Park, she reportedly commented to a Secret Service agent that the experience was good for him: "Unless he is allowed freedom, he'll be a vegetable." During his teens, Jackie sent him on an outward bound program on Hurricane Island, and a seventy-day survival course in Kenya.

She proudly succeeded in raising independent, spirited children. Caroline enjoyed riding but did not automatically share her mother's enthusiasms. When Jackie enrolled her in ballet classes, she quickly showed her lack of interest. She also refused to be a debutante when she came of age. Instead of going straight to Radcliffe College, Harvard, where she had been accepted, Caroline took a Fine Art course at Sotheby's in London. Caroline went on to fulfill her academic promise at Radcliffe, where she graduated in Fine Art in 1980, then joined the Office of Film and Television at the Metropolitan Museum of Art.

John's path was less straightforward—he graduated from Brown University in Rhode Island in 1983, but went on to fail his bar exams twice at New York University before taking a job in the Manhattan District Attorney's office in 1989. (Later, when Caroline took her bar exams, she passed first time.) John was a naturally talented performer, mimic, and magnetically good-looking (*People* magazine voted him "The Sexiest Man Alive" in 1988).

Jackie did not encourage him to pursue an acting career. She was not there to see him in the Brian Friel play, *Winners*, in 1985. "She identified with John—he was full of life and good humor, a constant spark," said her friend Joe Armstrong, "but she worried about him too. She knew he had leadership potential, but he was so charmingly casual all the time."

Caroline and John both readily took on the responsibility of representing their father's memory and continuing his work, appearing at public ceremonies, but neither was keen to take public office. As John commented, "I would want to make sure that was what I wanted to do, and that I didn't do it because people thought I should."

In 1986, Caroline wed intellectual Edwin Schlossberg, who was thirteen years her senior—the same age gap as between Jack and Jackie. Jackie approved of Caroline's choice of husband and trusted her opinion, too, when it came to the dress made by Carolina Herrera. "I am not going to be interfering because I had a very bad experience with my wedding. It was the dress that my mother wanted me to wear and I hated it."

Jackie became a grandmother in 1988 to Rose, who bore a remarkable resemblance to Jackie as a child with her dark, Bouvier hair and wide-set eyes. Rose was quickly followed by Tatiana and then John. The press called her "Granny O."; her grandchildren affectionately called her "Grand Jackie." Nancy Tuckerman remembers their visits to 1040 Fifth Avenue: "She was able to hold their attention for hours on end. They'd put on costumes they'd make from old scarves and bits of material. Jackie would then take them on a so-called fantasy adventure. She'd weave a spellbinding tale while leading them through the darkened apartment, opening closet doors in search of ghosts and mysterious creatures."

Jackie relished her times with them, her sense of fun and imagination had remained unchanged since she used to say to Caroline in the White House, "Let's go kiss the wind!"

Left: **Jackie with Caroline at the wedding of cousin Courtney Kennedy (daughter of Bobby) to Jeff Ruhe, June 14, 1980**

Jackie just loved John. When you mentioned John's name to Jackie, her voice became a gentle laugh ...

Karen Lerner

Previous page: **Jackie with Caroline, Teddy, and John at Caroline's graduation from Radcliffe College, Harvard, June 5, 1980**

Left: **Jackie, fifty-two, and John, twenty-two, walking together in a snowy Manhattan, February 1983**

She raised her kids ... (so) that all three locked onto each other in a way that families almost never do. They all came through for one another. She really liked them as friends.

Fred Papert

Right: **Jackie with Caroline at the inauguration of the statue of John F. Kennedy in Boston, May 29, 1990**

Jackie increasingly let her children take center stage at events relating to their father. Caroline had been in charge of commissioning the statue of John F. Kennedy.

My mother had never had an agenda for me or my sister. That's probably why we're all so close and have had a relatively normal life ... She has not made us look to our father's life to worship it at the expense of our own.

John F. Kennedy Jr.

Left: **Jackie with John at the Profile in Courage Awards held at the John F. Kennedy Library, May 1991**

Jackie, Caroline and John set up the award, named after John F. Kennedy's 1956 Pulitzer Prize-winning book, *Profiles in Courage*, to honor elected officials who had displayed particular valor.

Caroline felt strongly that her father represented the ideal of public service: "They joined the Peace Corps because of him; they worked in the inner cities because of him; they ran for office because he asked them to give something back to their country ..."

The children have been a wonderful gift to me and I'm thankful to have once more seen our world through their eyes. They restore my faith in the family's future.

Right: **Jackie with granddaughter Rose in Central Park, New York, June 18, 1992**

She could retreat and withdraw and I had seen her very cold to people—but she was capable of a very childlike intense sort of affection ... In that sense she was a very, very magnetic person.

Edna O'Brien

Left: Jackie watching Caroline and her four-year-old granddaughter, Tatiana, playing in the snow in Central Park, New York, March 1994

Finding love

Jackie's existence had been defined by her choice of men. The last and longest partnership in her life was the most equal of all her matches. She had no imperative to be with Maurice Tempelsman apart from her love for him.

Tempelsman was born in Belgium a month after Jackie, and was an Orthodox Jew whose family had escaped to America just prior to the Nazi occupation. He joined his father Leon's diamond merchant business and, by 1950, had created a key role for himself as a middleman between the African diamond marketers and the US government, to help the government stockpile diamonds for military and industrial purposes. He made contributions to Jack Kennedy's campaign in 1960, and he and his wife Lilly had been guests at the White House during Kennedy's presidency. His position in the diamond industry had made him extremely rich, and he rose to become one of the few "sightholders" in the world, with the right to buy diamonds direct from the De Beers' cartel.

He was still legally married to Lilly, a marriage counselor, when he began to spend more time with Jackie, in the late seventies. Jackie and Maurice's relationship did not make the headlines until the eighties—he was one of the least well known of her walkers, and cut an unassuming figure next to her out in Manhattan. She often referred to him as "M. T."

One magazine reported in 1976 that she had dined with "Max Tempelsman," who was described as a "New York jeweler."

Jackie said of him: "I admire Maurice's strength and his success. I truly hope my notoriety doesn't force him out of my life." Tempelsman offered her great companionship—they were on the same intellectual plane and had the same artistic enthusiasms. As well as a love of the theater and the ballet, he was a collector of Turkish and Greek artefacts and had wide knowledge of history and literature. One friend commented: "It was very strange, that relationship, because it wasn't earthy or even worldly. It was all sort of high culture."

With his astute financial sense, he could also fulfill the role of advisor, which Jackie's friend André Meyer had taken on until his death in 1979. He also was as interested as Jackie in protecting their privacy. He instigated the second court battle with Ron Galella in 1982, which resulted in Galella relinquishing all rights to photograph Jackie, John, and Caroline.

In 1982, Tempelsman's wife Lilly asked him to leave when it was clear that their marriage was effectively over. He moved into a suite at the Stanhope Hotel nearby and then into Jackie's apartment. Later, he obtained a "get" from his wife, so that under Jewish law they were no longer married. He kept in contact with Lilly and stayed close to his three children, after whom he named his yacht *Relemar*. Maurice and Jackie would cruise around Martha's Vineyard on *Relemar*.

Jackie's circle, apart from the notable exception of Bill Walton, approved of Maurice. "He was the nicest man she ever had, far and away," said her friend Aileen Mehle.

"He didn't regard her as a trophy," another friend, Tony Coelho, commented. Caroline and John, who were at first tentative in their acceptance of Tempelsman, grew attached to him when they observed the profound contentment he brought to their mother. Jackie helped him convalesce from a heart attack in the 1980s, and he took care of her as she suffered with the cancer that ended her life. Even days before she died, Jackie and Maurice were seen walking arm-in-arm together through Central Park.

Above: **Jackie on the cover of the *National Enquirer*, years after Maurice Tempelsman and his wife had separated, December 31, 1991**

Left: **Jackie with Maurice Tempelsman—she began dating him in 1975**
Unusually, she is photographed smoking in public—something she usually managed to avoid.

They were truly affectionate. When they looked at each other you could see they were terribly in love. But it was a love also offering great serenity.

Yolande Clergue, friend

Right: **A radiant Jackie with Maurice Tempelsman, New York, 1986**

The person we knew was someone who had ... already suffered terribly ... and who had enormously wisened, and who had gained in breadth and depth because of those miseries, and who had become much more herself. Cleansed by fire, but terrible fire.

Cary Welch, friend

Right: **Jackie reading on the hood of a car, at her home, Red Gate Farm, Martha's Vineyard, on her sixtieth birthday, July 28th 1989**

Next page: **The Kennedys and the Clintons aboard Maurice Tempelsman's yacht *Relemar*, Martha's Vineyard, August 24, 1993**

Jackie had long been a supporter of Bill Clinton, who had once met Jack in the Rose Garden at the White House. Jackie and John were two of the first contributors to his presidential campaign.

Jackie invited the Clintons to join them to celebrate Bill Clinton's birthday. "It was a glorious day," Hillary Clinton remembers. "We went out and traveled to all those little islands around the coast there, ending up anchored off a deserted island ... Then we swam for hours. She was a great swimmer. She didn't just hang around in the water, she swam toward the island, then got out and walked on the rocky shore."

Jackie admired Hillary's gumption in the White House: "America is getting a bargain with her. She's worth two Helen of Troys."

She went out with her usual courage and style

Maurice Tempelsman

Right: **Jackie and Maurice Tempelsman walking down Madison Avenue back to her Fifth Avenue apartment a week before she died. May 12, 1994**

Next page: **Jackie's coffin is carried from St. Ignatius Loyola Church in New York, watched by John, Caroline, Maurice Tempelsman, and Edwin Schlossberg, May 23, 1994**

Nancy Tuckerman organized the funeral at the same church where Jackie had been baptized and confirmed. The pallbearers were led by Jackie's long-serving Secret Service agent John Walsh.

Caroline read the poem "Memory of Cape Cod" by Edna St. Vincent Millay, from the book Jackie had won as a prize at Miss Porter's School, and Maurice Tempelsman recited "Ithaka" by C. P. Cavafy, using his own words to conclude:

"And now the journey is over.
Too short, alas, too short.
It was filled with adventure and wisdom,
laughter and love, gallantry and grace.
So farewell, farewell."

No one else looked like her, spoke like her, wrote like her, or was so original in the way she did things. No one else we knew ever had a better sense of self.

Teddy Kennedy, in his eulogy

She did it in her own way and in her own terms, and we all feel lucky for that, and now she's in God's hands

John F. Kennedy Jr.

Above: **On a street in Manhattan, one of Jackie's admirers pays tribute, May 23, 1994**

Interview with Yusha Auchincloss contd
JACKIE'S STEPBROTHER
Hammersmith Farm, December 2004

We had stayed in touch by letter all our lives, and tried to see each other when we could. In 1961, when the Kennedys came to Paris and Jackie made such a hit with de Gaulle and the French people, I was living in Cairo and flew up to see her. As a girl, Jackie loved dogs almost as much as horses. She also was a great admirer of war heroes, and named one of her childhood dogs 'Winston' after Winston Churchill, and the other, a French poodle, 'Gaullie' named after General de Gaulle.

I remember arriving at the official reception de Gaulle gave for Jack and Jackie at the Élysée Palace in Paris. De Gaulle was standing next to Jackie in the receiving line. I had not seen Jackie for a while as I was living abroad, and we were thrilled to see each other. I kissed her, because you don't shake hands with your sister. De Gaulle frowned, trying to figure out who this guy was going through the receiving line kissing his guest of honor. Jackie told him I was her beloved brother. Later, after dinner, we had a conversation, and I told him, 'My sister admired you so much as a girl, she named her French poodle after you.' There was a silence, when I could see Jackie wasn't sure how he was going to take it. But he was very appreciative and we all laughed. She was charming and laughter was what happened often when you were with Jackie.

How would Jackie want me to remember her? Caroline, her daughter, knew how close Jackie and I were, so just before she died, she invited me to spend some time alone with her, my sister, at her bedside. I told her that her support was still a source of strength to me. I recalled with gladness her life defined by a joy of living rather than the sorrow I felt at her passing. I told her of my gratitude for our friendship of the past and the pride I have at the memory of that friendship. I knew she would want me to reminisce of the happy times when we walked and talked and traveled together. When we hugged at our greetings and our *bientôts*.

I kissed her *au revoir* and held her hand for a moment, whispered in her ear to keep up her courage and heard her sigh, "Not to worry." She made me feel that she was already imagining, in a whimsical dream, a group of dancing angels preparing to greet her and reunite her with her father, husband, and children above the clouds and beyond the stars, each holding a stem of her favorite blue cornflower. As she lay there, she could still show that same impatient move of the head, soft breathing, and that firm touch she had exhibited as a champion equestrian. I knew that she realized it was time to go on, and she would not want to keep her Maker waiting. She left without self-pity, just as she had held back the tears that had flowed in her eyes in order to give strength and hope to countless others thirty-one years earlier.

chapter 6

Jackie the Icon

A lady of legend

From her first days as the President's wife, Jackie Kennedy's every move and sartorial choice contributed to her legendary image. Even after the monstrous shock of her husband's assassination, she purposefully set about disseminating the metaphor of Camelot to describe their days in the White House, in order to secure those years as a remarkable, magical period in American history.

Jackie, with her highbrow tastes and impeccable bearing, transformed the First Family into a youthful and glamorous American royalty. Subsequently, when she sabotaged the public conception of her as a symbol of spotless nobility by marrying Aristotle Onassis, her fame remained undimmed. She continued to carefully manage her own public face at the end of her life. For her final interview, which she granted to *Publisher's Weekly* (USA) in 1993—her first in thirty years—Jackie insisted on strict conditions, prohibiting the use of a tape recorder and insisting on quote approval. Predictably, she gave nothing away.

Her inscrutability during her lifetime nourished the sense of her importance. She purposefully used her secretive nature as a tool of attraction at times, but her friend Edna O'Brien interprets this condition as something less contrived:

"Distance and distancing were central to her, not only from others, but from huge parts of herself. It was what gave her that inexplicable aura. Her mystery was that she was a mystery to herself."

Despite her lack of encouragement, the enormous reach of Jackie's appeal was such that she could not prevent a bustling industry of products and services appearing which traded on her status and her style—dress-up dolls, knockoff dresses and pillbox hats, plastic surgeons offering the Jackie Kennedy nose. This attention was the wrong kind for Jackie; it was vulgar and she tried to resist it. In the early eighties, she brought (and won) a court case against the fashion house Christian Dior, which had photographed a Jackie lookalike, Barbara Reynolds, standing next to a Charles de Gaulle lookalike, for one of their advertisements.

Her unmatchable celebrity was perhaps most eloquently expressed by her sometime friend Andy Warhol, in over one hundred portraits he produced of her, both as smiling President's wife and stricken widow. However, the writer George Plimpton, who had known Jackie since her first trips to Paris, was emphatic that she did not tacitly crave such tributes. He said:

"That Andy Warhol did a portrait, that there was iconography— she was dismayed by it … she did not want a part of anything like that. Some famous people just glory in it, walking along the street, hoping to be recognized … There was nothing less a part of Jackie."

Jackie's life story, overburdened with mythic elements of both fairytale and tragedy, is enduringly compelling. The places she made her home in Washington and New York have become the main stops on Jackie-devoted tourist walking tours. For the most part of her life, and since her death, Jackie has been the subject of an unremitting stream of biographical examinations in print. Fascinated admirers, such as writer Wayne Koestenbaum, have tried to capture her essence—he refers to himself as one of her "constituents" and writes that "she seemed to have surreal powers of movement and metamorphosis."

Various well known actresses from Jacqueline Bisset to *Charlie's Angel* Jaclyn Smith have attempted to portray Jackie's character on stage, in films, and in TV mini-series.

Jackie has also predictably become a favorite subject for female impersonators, as the late Truman Capote observed at a Harlem contest. He reflected somewhat bitchily in his unfinished book *Answered Prayers*:

"A dozen boys … wore her high-rise hairdo, winged eyebrows, sulky, palely painted mouth. In life, that is how she struck me—not as a bona fide woman, but as an artful female impersonator impersonating Mrs. Kennedy."

Now, over a decade since her death, she is still seen as an exemplar of elegance. Her once much-imitated look may no longer dominate mainstream fashion, but Jackie remains an idol for major designers—Valentino still cries when he talks of her, and New York designer Michael Kors' respect for Jackie is such that his collections could often be described as homages to her jet-set chic.

She was conferred with an esthete's equivalent of a canonization when, in 2001, the Metropolitan Museum of Art in New York assembled a major retrospective of her clothes and other personal effects from the White House years.

Right: **Portrait of Jackie Kennedy Onassis by Aaron Shikler, 1968.**
This was begun in the late 1960s—another version now hangs in the White House alongside other eminent first ladies.

This is my Mommy.
She is very beautiful.
She is the most beautiful Mommy ever.
Color her beautiful.
See her pretty clothes?
They are very expensive.
They cost my daddy a lot of money.
Is that why he can't afford an overcoat?

Above: **A satirical coloring book devoted to the First Family, 1962.**

Left: **Jackie in her Inaugural ballgown, and Caroline in pajamas, immortalized as porcelain dolls, 1961.**

She was an image of beauty
and romance and she leaves
an empty place in the world as
I have known it

Lady Bird Johnson

Right: **A souvenir photo book devoted to Jacqueline Kennedy, 1964**

OVER 100
PICTURES

ONE DOZEN
RED ROSES
the life story of

ONE DOLLAR

JACQUELINE KENNEDY

COLLECTORS' ISSUE

Above: **Jacqueline Bisset as Liz Cassidy (an undisguised Jackie O) in the 1978 film, *The Greek Tycoon***

She starred opposite Anthony Quinn as the Onassis character, Theo Tomasis. Quinn was a friend of Jackie's, but she refused to speak to him after he took the role. Bisset has more recently played Jackie again, in the 2003 TBS television film *America's Prince: The John F Kennedy Jr. Story.*

Above: **Blair Brown made one of the more convincing Jackies when she starred opposite Martin Sheen in the 1983 TV series, *Kennedy*.**
She had grown up in Washington as the daughter of a CIA man and used to dress up as Jackie when she was a little girl.

My first impression—and it never changed—was that I was in the presence of a very great tragic actress ... Jacqueline Kennedy ... provided us with an unforgettable performance as the nation's heroine

William Manchester

Right: **Theater poster for *Jackie, A Satirical Comedy,* Queens Theater, London, October 1998**

A satirical drama of an American icon, the play was written and directed by Gip Hoppe and transferred to London from its sixteen-week run on Broadway, New York. In London it starred Lysette Anthony.

When in history has there been a First Lady so beautifully dressed and so wonderful to look at and so young?

Letitia Baldridge

Left: **Star lots of jewelry from Sotheby's sale, New York, April 1996**
Famous pieces of jewelry from the Jackie Kennedy Onassis estate sale, included: (left) a triple-strand necklace of simulated pearls, immortalized in the 1962 photograph of young John Jr. with his mother, which fetched $211,500 against its estimate of $700 to $900; (right) a black stone necklace that Jackie wore when her husband announced his candidacy for president, and on their trip to Paris in 1961, which sold for $101,500, and (center) the 40-carat diamond engagement ring from Aristotle Onassis which sold for $2.6 million.

Other lots included one of Jackie's French textbooks from Miss Porter's School; and her last car, a teal colored 1992 BMW with 10,032 miles on the odometer. Sotheby's conservatively estimated that the items on offer would be worth around $5 million, but the final total from the sale amassed $34,457,470, exceeding the previous record-breaking personal sales of Andy Warhol and The Duchess of Windsor.

TIME magazine described the sale and its accompanying hysteria as a "perverse tribute" to Jackie.

Caroline Kennedy decided to sell a second load of Kennedy property in February 2005, including monogrammed horse blankets and sketches by Bill Walton, from Jackie's various homes in Hyannis Port, Martha's Vineyard, New Jersey, New York City, and Virginia, donating a portion of the proceeds to the John F. Kennedy Library Foundation.

Right: **Outfits at the 2001 Metropolitan Museum of New York exhibition: "Jacqueline Kennedy The White House Years," which subsequently was shown in the John F. Kennedy Museum in Boston.**

Hamish Bowles, European editor-at-large of *American Vogue*, meticulously curated the exhibition which brought together a comprehensive collection of 80 evening gowns and day wear along with such White House relics as her seating plans for dinners and functions.

In the glass cases stood the bright red Pierre Cardin suit in which she greeted Canadian Mounties in Ottawa, the vividly embroidered Givenchy gown she wore to the unforgettable dinner at the Palace of Versailles, and the "liquid columnar" Grecian draped dress Oleg Cassini designed for the Nobel Prize Winners' dinner at the White House. "She was going for an understated effect with her clothes so that she herself was the dominant force," Bowles said.

The centerpiece of the exhibition was the Oleg Cassini ivory silk gown she wore to the Inauguration Gala on the eve of John F. Kennedy's Inauguration. Bowles describes the unfussy gown as "a masterstroke of image-making" —Jackie had seized her moment to visually define her role as the President's wife, youthful and dignified.

Image-making was the main endgame—in the exhibition, Bowles draws attention to noticing that some garments were not finished to anything like couture standards, but still fulfilled their purpose as striking and theatrical outfits designed to be seen by crowds and caught on camera.

The exhibition was a technicolor view of a wardrobe worthy of the Camelot legend, but lacked any acknowledgement of its tragic end, with no mention of the pink Chanel suit Jackie wore to Dallas or the black veil frantically produced by a White House maid which signaled her widowhood.

Oleg Cassini (b. France, 1913) after spring-summer
1962 model by Hubert de Givenchy (b. France, 1927)
Evening dress in pink silk chiffon embroidered
with porcelain beads and rhinestones, 1963
Opening of the "Mona Lisa" exhibition, National Gallery of
Art, Washington, D.C., January 8, 1963; state dinner honoring
Prasana Sarogballi Radhakrishnan of India, White House,
June 3, 1963

Givenchy's original design was an intriguing
synthesis of the sari—a fashion craze in the wake
of Mrs. Kennedy's India tour—and the ersatz
Edwardianism of My Fair Lady. Jacqueline Kennedy
wore this dress to the Washington exhibition of
the Mona Lisa. André Malraux, French minister of
culture, secured the painting as a personal loan to
Mrs. Kennedy—a triumph for Mrs. Kennedy,
"a regal reunion," noted LIFE, "and
her glowing best."

Interview with Michael Kors

THE NEW YORK FASHION DESIGNER, ON JACKIE AND HER UNIQUE STYLE

New York, January 2005

Michael Kors is a renowned American fashion designer specializing in luxury sportswear. His trademark is a sleek, sophisticated look, with a relaxed, understated elegance. In this interview, he describes the impact of Jackie's style on his own taste and fashion preferences.

Because of my age, I wasn't aware of Jackie as First Lady, but first fell in love with her look during the Ari years of the late Sixties when their exploits filled the newspapers and the news every day. Jackie and Ari Onassis were the ultimate jet-setters; forget about traveling by private plane—they had their own airline!

Jackie was a leader of fashion, but there was no one period when her style was more successful than another for me. With the eye of a great fashion editor, she worked every look from Fifties debutante to Sixties jet-setter to Seventies working gal pretty perfectly. A pair of large, dark Jackie sunglasses are still a traveler's best friend. Think about every person you've ever been in love with arriving at an airport—it's always about the sunglasses! And that's down to her. Also, she was one of the first women to realise that it was chic to wear couture with a bare leg—that was radical.

The three outfits which sum up the "Jackie" style that I personally love are:
1. Black short sleeve t-shirt, white jeans, and oversized glasses barefoot in Capri.
2. Suede jeans, long sleeve poor boy sweater, caught by camera on a New York City street.

3. In a sleeveless shift, bare legs, and Jack Rogers sandals going to church in Palm Beach.

Jackie's style has been a huge influence on my own as a fashion designer. Jackie combined the sporty and the elegant with a streamlined edge—three elements which are always significant in my clothes. In my recent collection for Summer 2005 I was definitely influenced by Jackie's Greek period of her life—what I call the Skorpios years.

The images of Jackie taken by Ron Gallella have also been very influential. The photograph of Jackie on the street, hair blowing, in her poor boy and jeans is just genius. Such style. Her sister has it too. I once sat next to Lee Radziwill on Concorde, and she was wearing a T-shirt and the perfect pants. And then she pulled out her cashmere scarf and told the flight attendant, "'I'll just have the caviar, thank you.'" Cashmere, caviar and the Concorde: a potent mix.

I met Jackie several times: when I worked at a 57th Street boutique called Lothar's as a teenager, I waited on her and sold her jeans and sweaters. I later remember being dazzled by her entrance to a party at the Metropolitan Museum in a white strapless McFadden gown.

Her lasting legacy as a fashion icon and continuing influence on me and the fashion world are timelessness, simplicity, and a sporty sense of elegance.

One of the most intelligent and elegant people I have ever known, with such a creative imagination and gift for using just the right phrase. And with everything else, very kind and thoughtful, loyal to her friends.

Kitty Galbraith

Left: **Jackie, Metropolitan Museum of Art, New York, 6 December 1976**
She wore this pleated gown by Mary McFadden to the opening of the "The Glory of Russian Costume" show at the Costume Institute of the Metropolitan Museum of Art. Jackie was closely involved with the staging of this exhibition, and edited the accompanying book.

Photo Credits

The Associated Press
pages 129 (Henry Burroughs), 226, 230, 250 (Eddie Adams), 342, 390–391

CORBIS
© **Corbis:** pages 120–121, 188, 238; © **Ginsburg Clifford Alan/Corbis Sygma:** page 393; © **Bettmann/Corbis:** pages 2, 13, 19, 21, 25, 44, 65, 78, 83, 84, 88, 100, 104, 106, 109, 110, 112–113, 119, 126, 130, 140, 145, 157, 158, 161, 166, 170, 171, 179, 183, 202–203, 208–209, 210, 233, 256–257, 264–265, 269, 270, 274, 277, 280, 285, 292, 295, 296, 299, 304, 313, 317, 334–335, 345, 349, 355, 360–361, 366–367, 407; © **Cecil Beaton/Condé Nast Archive/Corbis:** page 47; © **Randy Faris/Corbis:** page 79; **Brooks Kraft/Corbis:** pages 22, 278–279 (**Cecil Stoughton, U. S. Army Signal Corps/John Fitzgerald Kennedy Library**); © **Reuters/Corbis:** page 413

Ron Galella
Ron Galella/Ron Galella, Ltd.: page 330; **Joy Smith/Ron Galella, Ltd.** pages 326–327;

Getty Images
pages 244, 249, 273; **AFP/Getty Images:** pages 217, 410; **CBS Photo Archive/Getty Imges:** page 196; **Morgan Collection/Getty Images:** pages 8–9, 28, 29, 32, 133, 216; **Time Life Pictures/Getty Images:** pages 38–39, 56, 59, 63, 68, 70–71, 91, 99, 114, 136, 153, 162–163, 164, 176, 194, 195, 199, 237, 266, 359, 371, 402

John Fitzgerald Kennedy Library, Boston
pages 31, 35, 154; **Robert Knudsen, White House/John Fitzgerald Kennedy** Library: pages 148–149, 184–185, 200, 205; **Abbie Rowe, National Park Service/John Fitzgerald Kennedy Library:** page 139;

Quotation Credits

CHAPTER 1

p6 Roy Jenkins in *The Times*, 21 May 1994

p10 C David Heymann, *A Woman Named Jackie*, p19 (hereafter referred to as C David Heymann)

p11 C David Heymann p17; Sarah Bradford *America's Queen*, p3 (hereafter referred to as Sarah Bradford)

p15 Doris Kearns Goodwin, quoted in *People*, June 6 1994

p20 C David Heymann p28; Sarah Bradford p15

p21 Sarah Bradford p19

p23 C David Heymann p34

p24 C David Heymann p29

p26 C David Heymann p35

p27 John H Davis, *Jacqueline Bouvier: An Intimate Memoir*, (hereafter referred to as John H Davis); C David Heymann, p13; Sarah Bradford p10; Sarah Bradford, p50 (from an interview with Lee Radziwill)

p30 Carl Sferrazza Anthony, *As We Remember Her*, p18 (hereafter referred to as Carl Sferrazza Anthony, Carl Sferrazza Anthony, p17

p33 Carl Sferrazza Anthony, p16

p34 Carl Sferrazza Anthony, p30;

p40 Charlotte Curtis quoted in C David Heymann, p70; Columbus O'Donnell quoted in C David Heymann, p73; Sarah Bradford, p51 p41 C David Heymann, p82; Carl Sferrazza Anthony, p39; Sarah Bradford, p63

p43 Carl Sferrazza Anthony, p36

p45 Carl Sferrazza Anthony, p41

p46 Sarah Bradford, p83; Sarah Bradford, p67

CHAPTER 2

p50 Carl Sferrazza Anthony, p61 Carl Sferrazza Anthony, p63

p51 Sarah Bradford, p82; C David Heymann, p92

p52 Mary Van Rensslaer Thayer, *Jacqueline Bouvier Kennedy*, (hereafter referred to as Mary Van Rensslaer Thayer) quoted in Sarah Bradford p78; Sarah Bradford, p79; Carl Sferrazza Anthony, p74

p53 C David Heymann, p142; Gore Vidal, *Palimpsest, A Memoir*, p310 (hereafter referred to as Gore Vidal)

p54 C David Heymann, p126; C David Heymann, p146

p56 Carl Sferrazza Anthony, p79

p58 Carl Sferrazza Anthony, p77

p60 Sarah Bradford, p115; C David Heymann, p146

p61 C David Heymann, p116; Sarah Bradford, p123

p62 C David Heymann, p116–117; C David Heymann, p121; C David Heymann, p116

p69 C David Heymann, p132

p72 C David Heymann, p165–166; Carl Sferrazza Anthony, p102

p73 Carl Sferrazza Anthony, p101

p76 Orlando Suero/Anne Garside, *Camelot at Dawn*, (excerpted in *John Hopkins Magazine*, Nov 2001)

p77 C David Heymann, p167

p78 C David Heymann, p17; *Sports Illustrated*, Dec 26, 1960

p82 C David Heymann, p195

p85 Carl Sferrazza Anthony, p89; Truman Capote quoted in C David Heymann, p177

p87 From Mary Van Rensslaer Thayer, quoted in Sarah Bradford p201

p89 Carl Sferrazza Anthony, p107

p90 Carl Sferrazza Anthony, p107; from Mary Van Rensslaer Thayer

p94 Sarah Bradford, p182; Carl Sferrazza Anthony, p113; C David Heymann, p211; C David
Heymann, p217; Sarah Bradford, p175; C David Heymann, p238; C David Heymann, p241

p97 C David Heymann, p220

p98 From a letter to Yusha Auchincloss, C David Heymann, p208

p101 C David Heymann, p201

p102 C David Heymann, p210

p105 Carl Sferrazza Anthony, p109

p107 Carl Sferrazza Anthony, p118

p108 Sally Bedell Smith, *Grace And Power*, p7, (hereafter referred to as Sally Bedell Smith)

p111 Carl Sferrazza Anthony, p109

p115 Sally Bedell Smith, p8

p118 Sally Bedell Smith, p8

CHAPTER 3

p122 Sally Bedell Smith, p90; Sally Bedell Smith, p133

p123 Sally Bedell Smith p135; Sally Bedell Smith p144; Carl Sferrazza Anthony p170
Norman Mailer, *The Presidential Papers*, p112 (hereafter referred to as Norman Mailer)

p124 Gore Vidal, p371; C David Heymann, p266; Sarah Bradford p273

p125 Sally Bedell Smith p155; Sarah Bradford p359

p127 Sarah Bradford p219

p128 Sally Bedell Smith p63

p131 Sally Bedell Smith p70

p137 Sally Bedell Smith p90

p138 C David Heymann, p266

p141 Sally Bedell Smith p114

p142 MMA, *Jacqueline Kennedy: The White House Years, Selections from the John F. Kennedy Library and
Museum*, p20 (hereafter referred to as MMA); MMA, p30

p143 Oleg Cassini, *A Thousand Days of Magic*, p30; C David Heymann, p25; Sarah Bradford p197

p144 Carl Sferrazza Anthony, p134; Oleg Cassini, *In My Own Fashion*, p316;
The Daily Telegraph, 5 April 1962; MMA, p17

p147 C David Heymann, p269

p150 *TIME*, 9 June 196; Carl Sferrazza Anthony, p150

p151 Carl Sferrazza Anthony, p152; Sarah Bradford, p293

p152 Carl Sferrazza Anthony, p148

p155 *TIME*, 9 June 1961; Carl Sferrazza Anthony, p150

p156 Carl Sferrazza Anthony, p151

p159 Carl Sferrazza Anthony, p151

p160 Sarah Bradford, p269

p165 from *The New York Times* quoted in Carl Sferrazza Anthony, p156; C David Heymann, p338

p167 C David Heymann, p349

p168 Sarah Bradford, p295

p170 Sarah Bradford, p293

p173 Oleg Cassini, *A Thousand Days of Magic*, p121

p177 Sally Bedell Smith, p267

p183 Sarah Bradford, p305

p186 C David Heymann, p266

p189 Carl Sferrazza Anthony, p182

p190 C David Heymann, p251

p191 Sally Bedell Smith, p22; Sally Bedell Smith, p97

p192 *The Daily Telegraph*, 4 August 1961

p193 *LIFE*, 1 September 1961; Norman Mailer, p109; Sarah Bradford, p255

p197 Sally Bedell Smith, p94; Sally Bedell Smith, p252

p198 Carl Sferrazz Anthony, p130

p200 Carl Sferrazza Anthony, p168

p204 Sally Bedell Smith, p92

p206 *The Daily Telegraph*, December 1961; Sally Bedell Smith, p107

p207 J.B. West, *Upstairs at the White House*, p200

p211 Carl Sferazza Anthony, p157

p214 Sally Bedell Smith, p291

p218 Sally Bedell Smith, p 106

p221 Sally Bedell Smith, p92

p222 C David Heymann, p265; Sally Bedell Smith, p106

p224 Carl Sferrazza Anthony, p189

p227 Carl Sferrazza Anthony, p193

p228 Carl Sferrazza Anthony, p193

p231 C David Heymann, p391

p232 Sarah Bradford, p351

p235 Sarah Bradford, p342; Sarah Bradford, p352

p236 Carl Sferrazza Anthony, p199; Sarah Bradford, p353

p238 Carl Sferrazza Anthony, p200

p241 Carl Sferrazza Anthony, p201

p242 Lady Bird Johnson, *A White House Diary*, p4

p243 Sally Bedell Smith, p443; Sarah Bradford p369

p248 Sally Bedell Smith, p444; Sarah Bradford, p379

p251 Sally Bedell Smith, p458; C David Heymann, p419

p252 Carl Sferrazza Anthony, p211

CHAPTER 4

p258 Carl Sferrazza Anthony, p213; Carl Sferrazza Anthony, p215

p259 *LOOK*, 17 November 1964; Carl Sferrazza Anthony, p228

p262 C David Heymann, p452; C David Heymann, p477

p263 C David Heymann, p493; C David Heymann, p558
p267 Carl Sferrazza Anthony, p212; James Spada, *Jackie, Her Life In Pictures*, p93
p268 C David Heymann, p426; C David Heymann, p429
p271 Carl Sferrazza Anthony, p231
p272 Sarah Bradford, p424
p275 C David Heymann, p445
p276 C David Heymann, p456
p281 Sarah Bradford, p534
p284 Carl Sferrazza Anthony, p233; Carl Sferrazza Anthony, p232
p286 Sarah Bradford, p394; C David Heymann, p429; Sarah Bradford, p534;
   Carl Sferrazza Anthony, p228;
p287 Carl Sferrazza Anthony, p86; Peter Evans, *Nemesis,* p125 (hereafter referred to as Peter Evans);
   C David Heymann, p 466
p288 Peter Evans, p124; C David Heymann, p482; Peter Evans, p122; Sarah Bradford, p446
p291 Carl Sferrazza Anthony, p210
p293 Gore Vidal, p311; Peter Evans, p168; Sarah Bradford, p432
p294 Carl Sferrazza Anthony, p236
p297 C David Heymann, p485
p298 Carl Sferrazza Anthony, p237
p300 Pamela Clarke Keogh, *Jackie Style*, p155 (hereafter referred to as Pamela Clarke Keogh)
p301 Pamela Clarke Keogh, p177; C David Heymann, p513; C David Heymann, p538
p302 C David Heymann, p512; Pamela Clarke Keogh, p177
p306 Carl Sferrazza Anthony, p240; Carl Sferrazza Anthony, p241; C David Heymann, p498;
   Vogue, December 1968
p307 Peter Evans, p188
p308 Carl Sferrazza Anthony, p252; Carl Sferrazza Anthony, p254
p310 Carl Sferrazza Anthony, p251; C David Heymann, p546; Carl Sferrazza Anthony, p25
p315 C David Heymann, p486; Carl Sferrazza Anthony, p248
p318 Sarah Bradford, p458
p321 C David Heymann, p565; Sarah Bradford, p499
p332 C David Heymann, p526

CHAPTER 5
p336 Carl Sferrazza Anthony, p275; Carl Sferrazza Anthony, p311
p337 C David Heymann, p596; C David Heymann, p552; Carl Sferrazza Anthony, p297
p338 Carl Sferrazza Anthony, p289
p339 Carl Sferrazza Anthony, p305; Carl Sferrazza Anthony, p298; Sarah Bradford, p575
p340 Carl Sferrazza Anthony, p350; Carl Sferrazza Anthony, p350; Sarah Bradford, p589
p343 Sarah Bradford, p557
p344 Carl Sferrazza Anthony, p301
p347 Sarah Bradford, p505
p348 Carl Sferrazza Anthony, p283
p351 Pamela Clarke Keogh, p233
p352 Letitia Baldridge, Interview with the author
C David Heymann, p573

C David Heymann, p573

Carl Sferrazza Anthony, p272

p353 Carl Sferrazza Anthony, p280; *People,* June 6 1994

p354 Carl Sferrazza Anthony, p327; Carl Sferrazza Anthony, p286; Sarah Bradford, p551; Sarah Bradford, p580

p355 C David Heymann, p575

p357 Pamela Clarke Keogh, p211; Pamela Clarke Keogh, p212

p358 C David Heymann, p609; Carl Sferrazza Anthony, p274

p362 Sarah Bradford p565

p363 Sarah Bradford, p538; Sarah Bradford, p583

p365 Sarah Bradford, p572; Sarah Bradford, p567; Carl Sferrazza Anthony, p316

p369 Sarah Bradford, p570

p370 Carl Sferrazza Anthony, p315

p373 Sarah Bradford, p565; Sarah Bradford, p583

p374 Pamela Clarke Keogh, p239

p377 Sarah Bradford, p581

p378 C David Heymann, p602

p379 Sarah Bradford, p562; Carl Sferrazza Anthony, p302

p382 Carl Sferrazza Anthony, p302

p384 Sarah Bradford, p578; Carl Sferrazza Anthony, p344; Carl Sferrazza Anthony, p330

p388 Sarah Bradford, p593

p392 Carl Sferrazza Anthony, p355

CHAPTER 6

p398 Sarah Bradford, p581

p399 Carl Sferrazza Anthony, p331; Wayne Koestenbaum *Jackie Under My Skin: Interpreting an Icon*

p400 Truman Capote, *Answered Prayers*, p153

p408 Sarah Bradford, p402

p410 Interview with CBS News 29 April 2001

p417 Sarah Bradford, p418

Bibliography

As We Remember Her, Carl Sferazza Anthony, Harper Collins, 2003

First Ladies, Volume II: The Saga of the President's Wives and their Power 1961–1990, William Morrow, 1991

In the Kennedy Style: Magical Evenings in the Kennedy White House, Letitia Baldridge, Doubleday, 1998

Of Diamond and Diplomats, Letitia Baldrige, Houghton Mifflin, 1968

Jacqueline Bouvier Kennedy Onassis, Stephen Birmingham, Grosset & Dunlap, 1978

America's Queen, A Life of Jacqueline Kennedy Onassis, Sarah Bradford, Viking, 2000

The Kennedy Women, Pearl S Buck, Cowles, 1970

Answered Prayers, Truman Capote, Penguin Classics, 2001

In My Own Fashion, Oleg Cassini, Pocket Books, 1987

A Thousand Days of Magic, Oleg Cassini, Rizzoli, 1995

Jacqueline Bouvier: An Intimate Memoir, John H Davis, Wiley, 1996

Nemesis, Peter Evans. Regan Books, 2004

Ari: The Life and Times of Aristotle Socrates Onassis, Peter Evans, Summit Books, 1986

Jacqueline, Ron Galella, Sheed and Ward, 1974

My Life with Jacqueline Kennedy, Mary Barelli Gallagher, New York: D. McKay Co., 1969

The Fitzgeralds and The Kennedys, Doris Kearns Goodwin, Simon & Schuster, 1987

A Woman Named Jackie, C David Heymann, Lyle Stuart, 1989

Jackie Oh!, Kitty Kelley, Mayflower Books, Granada Publishing, 1978

Jackie Style, Pamela Clarke Keogh, Harper Collins, 2001

All Too Human, Edward Klein, Pocket Books, 1997

Just Jackie: Her Private Years, Edward Klein, Ballantine, 1998

Jackie Under My Skin: Interpreting an Icon, Wayne Koestenbaum, Fourth Estate, 1996

The Presidential Papers, Norman Mailer, Penguin 1968

The Death of a President, William Manchester, Harper and Row, 1967

Jacqueline Kennedy: The White House Years, Selections from the John F Kennedy Library and Museum, MM, 2001

I was Jacqueline Kennedy's Dressmaker, Mimi Rhea, Fleet, 1962

Jackie Her Life in Pictures, James Spada, St Martin's Press, 2001

Grace and Power, Sally Bedell Smith, Random House, 2004

A Thousand Days: John F Kennedy in the White House, Arthur M Schlesinger, Houghton-Mifflin, 1965

Camelot at Dawn, Orlando Suero & Anne Garside, John Hopkins University Press, 2001

Palimpsest, A Memoir, Gore Vidal, pPenguin Books, 1995

Upstairs at the White House, J.B. West with Mary Lynn Kotz, W.H. Allen, 1974

Index

Page references in *italics* indicate illustration captions

First published by MQ Publications Limited
12 The Ivories
6–8 Northampton Street
London, N1 2HY
email: mqpublications.com
website: www.mqpublications.com

ISBN (10): 1-84072-677-6
ISBN (13): 978-1-84072-677-0

10 9 8 7 6 5 4 3 2

Printed in China

Nov 25 —	Jackie Kennedy leads the mourners at John F. Kennedy's funeral in Washington
Nov 29 —	Jackie grants interview at Hyannis Port to *Life* journalist Theodore White, and coins the metaphor of Camelot
Dec 6 —	Jackie and her children leave the White House and move into Governor Averell Harriman's home, 3036 N Street

★ **1964**

March —	Jackie gives evidence to the Warren Commission hearings investigating her husband's assassination
May 29 —	Jackie lays flowers with her children on Jack's grave at Arlington Cemetery to mark what would have been his 47th birthday.
July 7 —	Jackie announces she will be moving permanently to New York City. In the Fall she moved into an apartment at 1040 Fifth Avenue
Aug 27 —	Jackie appears at a reception at the Democratic Party Convention in Atlantic City; John F. Kennedy was commemorated in a series of speeches and readings.

★ **1965**

May 14 —	Jackie, Caroline and John attend dedication of the John F. Kennedy memorial by Queen Elizabeth at Runnymede, England

★ **1966**

Dec —	Jackie sues William Manchester to attempt to prevent the publication of his previously authorized account of the assassination *Death of a President.*

★ **1967**

June —	Jackie, Caroline and John spend a six week holiday in Ireland, visiting the Kennedy's town of origin Dunganstown
Nov —	Jackie Kennedy pays a semi-official visit to Cambodia and Thailand with Lord Harlech

★ **1968**

Mar 16 —	Bobby Kennedy announces his Presidential candidacy
Mar —	Jackie travels to Mexico with Deputy Secretary of State for Defense, Roswell Gilpatric, to see the archeological digs
April 7 —	Jackie attends the funeral of Dr Martin Luther King in Atlanta
May 25 —	Jackie joins On*assis*' yacht *Christina* cruising in the Caribbean. It is rumored Onassis proposed marriage on this holiday
June 5 —	Bobby Kennedy is assassinated by Palestinian gunman Sirhan Sirhan minutes after winning the California State Primary
June 8 —	Jackie Kennedy attends Bobby's funeral at St Patrick's Cathedral, New York
Oct 20 —	Jackie weds Aristotle Onassis on Skorpios

★ **1969**

Nov 18 —	Joseph P. Kennedy dies

★ **1972**

Feb 16 - Mar 23 —	Jackie fights a court case against paparazzi photographer Ron Galella and obtains an injunction so he cannot come near her or her children

★ **1973**

Jan 22 —	Alexander Onassis is killed when his hydroplane crashes

★ **1974**

Nov —	Aristotle Onassis is diagnosed with the incurable condition *myasthenia gravis*

★ **1975**

Jan —	Jackie telephones the offices of New York Municipal Arts Society offering her help in the battle to save Grand Central Station
Mar 15 —	Aristotle Onassis dies in Paris
Mar 18 —	Jackie attends the funeral of Aristotle Onassis on Skorpios